Religion
and the Law

Religion and the Law

Of Church and State and the Supreme Court

Philip B. Kurland

AldineTransaction
A Division of Transaction Publishers
New Brunswick (U.S.A.) and London (U.K.)

First paperback printing 2009
Copyright © 1961, 1962 by Philip B. Kurland.

All rights reserved under International and Pan-American Copyright Conventions. No part of this book may be reproduced or transmitted in any form or by any means, electronic or mechanical, including photocopy, recording, or any information storage and retrieval system, without prior permission in writing from the publisher. All inquiries should be addressed to AldineTransaction, A Division of Transaction Publishers, Rutgers—The State University, 35 Berrue Circle, Piscataway, New Jersey 08854-8042. www.transactionpub.com

This book is printed on acid-free paper that meets the American National Standard for Permanence of Paper for Printed Library Materials.

Library of Congress Catalog Number: 2008039940
ISBN: 978-0-202-36304-2
Printed in the United States of America

Library of Congress Cataloging-in-Publication Data

Kurland, Philip B.
  Religion and the law : of church and state and the Supreme Court /
Philip B. Kurland.
      p. cm.
  "Originally published: Chicago : Aldine Pub. Co., [1962]."
  Includes bibliographical references.
  ISBN 978-0-202-36304-2
    1. Church and state--United States. I. Title.

KF4865.K87 2009
342.7308'52--dc22

                              2008039940

To Mary Jane and our parents

PREFACE

The election of a Catholic as President of the United States and the excitement over the proposed national aid-to-education bills have raised the debate over the proper relationship between church and state, God and Caesar, religion and law, to an unprecedented crescendo in this country.

The subject is hardly a new one. Probably in prehistoric times, as among primitive peoples today, frequent power conflicts arose between the medicine man and the chief. Certainly the problem was known to the Greeks and the Romans, though merger of the contestants frequently muted the issues. It provided the dominant theme for six hundred years of European history. The very slow development of the notion of religious toleration and the absence of any notion of separation of church and state in the English speaking world outside of America, both before and after the American Revolution, amply demonstrate the continued vitality of the problem, with dimensions until now unknown in America. Thus, for example, it may surprise some that, by law, religious qualifications for public office in England continued late into the nineteenth century. And perhaps equally disquieting is the fact that the ultimate arbiter of Anglican church doctrine is, even today, not any ecclesiastical authority but the English Parliament, most of whose members are not actively affiliated with the Anglican church.

However hoary the problem, it is livelier than ever in the United States today. Federal aid to Catholic schools has become the essential issue on which many Congressional elections may turn: in the cities of the Northeast, the newly-formed Citizens Party, joined with a group called "Citizens for Educational Freedom," threatens to unseat or defeat any candidate who is not prepared to pledge himself to support federal contributions to parochial schools. Several congressmen have recently introduced a proposed amendment to the Constitution that would require recognition of "the authority and law of Jesus Christ, Saviour and ruler of nations, through

7

whom are bestowed the blessings of Almighty God." The problem has colored even the complexities of our foreign relations: President Kennedy recently announced that religion "is the issue which separates us from those who make themselves our adversary." Shortly thereafter, Brooks Hays, assistant to the President, announced that "the nonreligious description of foreign affairs is only a surface view." The notion of a holy war has hardly been heard in recent years except in the "backward" countries of northeast Africa and southwest Asia; it is, therefore, somewhat frightening to hear its echo in American foreign policy as announced by the President of the United States and his staff. The United States has been fortunate in keeping the strife of the church-state conflict to a minimum. No small contribution to this peaceful co-existence has been made by the Constitution and by the Supreme Court's readings of the First Amendment. It is to be wished, devoutly if you will, that the doleful experiences of countries lacking such safeguards shall forever remain foreign to us.

It is not surprising, however, in the context of current events that discussion of the issue of church and state rages everywhere in this country. Even before national attention was called to the problem, scholars were engaged in their great dialogue on the subject. On more mundane levels, the topic fills the newspapers and magazines, the austere columns of *The New York Times* no less than the pietistic pages of *Time*. Sunday sermons and barbershop conversations are similarly dedicated. People's feelings on the subject tend to run deep, with the almost inevitable consequence that their thinking about it tends to be shallow.

One of the fundamental difficulties with the contemporary discussion has been the failure to distinguish two separable problems: the constitutional issue—in the narrow sense of the meaning to be given to the language of the First Amendment by the Supreme Court—and the broader question of the ideal relationship that should exist between the two institutions contesting sovereignty over so much of man's actions, speech, and thoughts. Not only have emotion and reason produced a conflict that has blunted the distinction between constitutionality and desirability, but so, too, have expediency and responsibility been in opposition, with the same result. Thus, however politic it may be and have been for the President not to seek aid for parochial schools from Congress, there was little or no warrant for his proposition that the Supreme Court had by decision specifically precluded such action.

The contents of this volume are devoted solely to the constitutional question: the meaning and application of the religion clauses of the First Amendment, as construed by our highest judicial authority, the Supreme Court of the United States. (It should be noted, Tocqueville and others to the contrary notwithstanding, that not all important constitutional questions get to the Supreme Court for resolution.) Others have attempted such an assay, but they were writing briefs and their efforts are tainted by the goals of their clients. The Department of Health, Education and Welfare filed a document with the Senate purporting to demonstrate—in support of the President's dictum—that the decisions of the Court would preclude aid to parochial schools. An equally impressive but equally biased study by the Legal Department of the National Catholic Welfare Conference not unexpectedly reached the opposite conclusion. As a matter of fact, the materials that follow do not purport to offer any judgment on the question of federal aid to parochial schools. They do purport to present an analysis of the cases on the basis of which a judgment can be made as to what the law is likely to be, if the problem of parochial school aid or a similar question comes to the Court for decision.

The distinction between the issues of constitutionality and desirability is perhaps best expressed in personal terms. My own reading of the cases leads me to the conclusion that aid to parochial schools is not unconstitutional, so long as it takes a nondiscriminatory form. I am at least equally convinced that the segregation of school children by religion is an unmitigated evil. As a judge, I should have to vote to sustain the constitutionality of such legislation; as a legislator, I should have to vote against its passage. In light of my objective to isolate the constitutional issues, the reader is requested to keep in mind three relevant dicta essential to understanding the analysis that follows. The first is that of Holmes: "The truth is, that the law is always approaching and never reaching, consistency. It is forever adapting new principles from life at one end, and it always retains old ones from history at the other, which have not yet been absorbed or sloughed off. It will become entirely consistent only when it ceases to grow." The second is by Cardozo: "One of the most fundamental social interests is that law should be uniform and impartial." The last comes from Brandeis: "We must be ever on guard lest we erect our prejudices into legal principles."

Finally, it would seem desirable that, if he is to make a judgment on the basis of this essay, the reader be advised in advance of my "prejudices" in order to assure himself that I have not attempted to "erect" them "into legal principles." I believe that dogma—whether it be that of a religion or that of a political party or that of an economic school—is anathema to liberty and freedom and especially to liberty of thought. Although I have accepted much that Father John Courtney Murray has proposed as historical truth in his excellent book, *We Hold These Truths,* I reject his notion that "there is an authority superior to the authority of individual reason." I reject, too, his proposition that "by divine ordinance this world is to be ruled by a dyarchy of authorities, within which the temporal is subordinate

to the spiritual." Certainly the Constitution contemplates no such subordination of state to church. And I reject his theme, stated thus: "Society is
rescued from chaos only by a few men, not by the many. *Paucis humanum
vivit genus.* It is only the few who understand the disciplines of civility and
are able to sustain them in being and thus hold in check the forces of
barbarism that are always threatening to force the gates of the City."
I do not find in democracy the most felicitous answers to all political problems, but it has the happy attribute of affording freedoms that are absent
from all other forms of government that we have known.

I choose, therefore to cast my lot with Learned Hand: "For myself it
would be irksome to be ruled by a bevy of Platonic Guardians, even if
I knew how to choose them, which I assuredly do not." I do know that
I should certainly not choose them on the basis of their self-proclaimed
divine inspiration, for as Mr. Shirer has amply documented in *The Rise
and Fall of the Third Reich,* this "divine leadership" concept has already
cost the world too heavily in this century. Like Judge Hand, I read the
provisions of the Bill of Rights as "the altogether human expression of the
will of the state conventions that ratified them. . . . Their authority depends
upon the sanctions available to enforce them; and their meaning is to be
gathered from the words they contain, read in the historical setting in which
they were uttered. This presupposes that all political power emanates from
the people." This presupposition underlies all that follows in this book.

PHILIP B. KURLAND

CONTENTS

PART ONE

A Doctrine

in Search of Authority

INTRODUCTION

THERE ARE few issues so likely to generate heat rather than light as the question of the proper line between the realm of the state and that of the church. And yet, with the gratuitous courage they so often displayed, the framers of the Constitution's Bill of Rights began their blueprint for freedom by drawing exactly such a line. The first clauses of the first amendment provide: "Congress shall make no law respecting an establishment of religion or prohibiting the free exercise thereof." If this language is, to some, reminiscent of words of Delphi's Pythia, it should be remembered that they were not uttered until after provision had been made for priests to make the words meaningful for those who had to know their meaning. Nor have these justices of the Supreme Court been wanting in advice from self-appointed guardians. "The difficulty [with the advice] in this field, as in so many other fields of constitutional controversy, is that the contestants are more convincing when they criticize their opponents' interpretations than when they seek to establish the validity of their own . . . ."[1] It is the function of this essay to examine, not the theories of the commentators, but rather the actions and words of the Supreme Court in applying the constitutional language to the controversies that have come before it. Lest such a piece be reduced to what Thomas Reed Powell used to label "mere recitativo," however, these cases will also be measured against a "neutral principle" that, it is suggested, will give the most appropriate scope to the religion clauses in such a manner as to provide guidance for the legislatures and courts that are required to abide by the constitutional command. This "neutral principle" has been framed in reliance on the Aristotelian axiom that "it is the mark of an educated man to seek precision in each class of things just so far as the nature of the subject admits," rather than the Platonic precept that "a perfectly simple principle can never be applied to a state of things which is the reverse of simple."

15

1

A DOCTRINE

IN SEARCH OF AUTHORITY

Like most commands of our Constitution, the religion clauses of the first amendment are not statements of abstract principles. History, not logic, explains their inclusion in the Bill of Rights; necessity, not merely morality, justifies their presence there. As Father John Courtney Murray has noted: "Every historian who has catalogued the historical factors which made for religious liberty and separation of church and state in America would doubtless agree that these institutions came into being under the pressure of their necessity for the public peace."[2]

The factors creating this necessity were four, according to Murray.[3] The first was the large number of unbelievers in the community that inserted these guarantees into the Constitution.[4] The second was the great variety of denominations among the believers.[5] Third was the economic factor: "Persecution and discrimination were as bad for business affairs as they were for the affairs of the soul."[6] And last, and least in Murray's estimate, was the influence of the "widening religious freedom in England." There was a fifth of which Murray took no note, but which Professor Jordan put this way:

> [I]t seems apparent that very considerable gains had been made in terms of human decency, that men had come to be animated by an increasing sensitivity to human pain and suffering. This significant and obscure development . . . contributed most immediately and notably to the rise of religious toleration. It might be suggested, indeed, that the history of culture can in one sense be interpreted in terms of the rising and falling curve of man's sensitivity to cruelty and of his reaction to needless suffering. There was in religious persecution a very considerable and a very ugly psychological and moral element which must be described as sadism. Innate barbarism relieved and justified itself by the infliction of suffering for what was conceived as a moral end. . . . [T]he mass of men in England came to make a very sharp and important distinction between punishment imposed

16

for the judicially demonstrable fact of crime and the infliction of punishment for the retention of opinion. This must be regarded as one of the most significant cultural gains in human history. These gains of the human race are painfully and slowly attained and they may be lost before the mass of men realize that they are threatened. Brutality and sadism are deeply rooted in man's nature. They are restrained by no surer sanction than a decent attitude toward the fact of difference, which man's biological nature apparently teaches him to abhor but which his history has taught him he must respect in the interest of sheer survival.[7]

Religious toleration, summed up in the second of the two clauses, was, therefore, necessary to preserve the peace. Separation, represented by the first of the two clauses, was necessary to make such religious freedom a reality. But the separation clause had a greater function than the assurance of toleration of dissenting religious beliefs and practices. To suggest but two lessons of the evils resulting from the alliance of church and state, there was abundant evidence of the contributions of the churches to the warfare among nations as well as the conflict within them and equally obvious was the inhibition on scientific endeavor that followed from the acceptance by the state of church dogma. It is not necessary to suggest that the Francophiles in the American community were dedicated to the anti-clericalism that contributed to the French Revolution, but they certainly were not ignorant of the evils that aroused such violent reactions. For them toleration could hardly satisfy the felt needs; separation was a necessary concomitant. But admittedly separation was a new concept in practice. Toleration had a long English history; separation—conceived in the English writings of Roger Williams—had its beginnings as an historical fact only on the shores of this continent.[8] It is justified in Williams' terms by the necessity for keeping the state out of the affairs of the church, lest the church be subordinated to the state; in Jeffersonian terms its function is to keep the church out of the business of government, lest the government be subordinated to the church. Limited powers of government were not instituted to expand the realm of power of religious organizations, but rather in favor of freedom of action and thought by the people.

Nor were these two concepts closed systems at the time of the adoption of the first amendment. The objectives of the provisions were clear, but the means of their attainment were still to be developed and, indeed, are still in the course of development. Thus, like the other great clauses of the Constitution, the religion clauses cannot now be confined to the application they might have received in 1789.

The utilization or application of these clauses in conjunction is difficult. For if the command is that inhibitions not be placed by the state on religious activity, it is equally forbidden the state to confer favors upon religious activity. These commands would be impossible of effectuation unless they are read together as creating a doctrine more akin to the reading of the equal protection clause than to the due process clause, *i.e.*, they must be read to mean that religion may not be used as a basis for classification for purposes of governmental action, whether that action be the conferring of rights or privileges or the imposition of duties or obligations. Or, to put it in Lord Bryce's terms: "It is accepted as an axiom by all Americans that the civil power ought to be not only neutral and impartial as between different forms of faith, but ought to leave these matters entirely on one side. . . ."[9] It must be recognized, however, that this statement of the "neutral" principle of equality, that religion cannot supply a basis for classification of governmental action, still leaves many problems unanswered. Not the least of them flows from the fact that the actions of the state must be carefully scrutinized to assure that classifications that purport to relate to other matters are not really classifications in terms of religion.[10] "[C]lassification in abstract terms can always be carried to the point at which, in fact, the class singled out consists only of particular known persons or even a single individual. It must be admitted that, in spite of many ingenious attempts to solve this problem, no entirely satisfactory criterion has been found that would always tell us what kind of classification is compatible with equality before the law."[11]

It is the genius of the common law, and thus of American constitutional law,[12] that its growth and principles are measured in terms of concrete factual situations, or at least with regard to factual situations as concrete as the deficiencies of our adversary system permit them to be. It remains then to examine the cases that have arisen and the rationales offered in their solution and to see how the suggested thesis would resolve them. Before doing so, however, it might be desirable to repeat two propositions. First, the thesis proposed here as the proper construction of the religion clauses of the first amendment is that the freedom and separation clauses should be read as a single precept that government cannot utilize religion as a standard for action or inaction because these clauses prohibit classification in terms of religion either to confer a benefit or to impose a burden. Second, the principle offered is meant to provide a starting point for solutions to problems brought before the Court, not a mechanical answer to them.

PART TWO

Authorities

in Search of a Doctrine

2

THE EARLY MORMON CASES

The Supreme Court's concern with the religion clauses of the first amendment begins, for all practical purposes,[13] with the case of *Reynolds v. United States*,[14] where the Court first adopted the Jeffersonian statement that the amendment erected "a wall of separation between church and State."[15] The case arose in the context of a general "hostility to Mormonism [that] was due not merely to the practice of polygamy, but also to the notion that the hierarchy of the Latter Day Saints constituted a secret and tyrannical *imperium in imperio* opposed to the genius of democratic institutions."[16] *Reynolds* raised the question whether a statute of the United States that made polygamy illegal could be constitutionally applied to a Mormon. At the trial, the court had refused Reynolds' request to instruct the jury that "if he was married . . . in pursuance of and in conformity with what he believed at the time to be a religious duty . . . the verdict must be 'not guilty.' "[17] Instead the judge had told the jury that if the defendant "deliberately married a second time, having a first wife living" the fact that he did so "under the influence of a religious belief that it was right,—under an inspiration, if you please, that it was right," did not relieve him of criminal liability:

> Upon this charge and refusal to charge the question is raised, whether religious belief can be accepted as a justification of an overt act made criminal by the law of the land. The inquiry is not as to the power of Congress to prescribe criminal laws for the Territories, but as to the guilt of one who knowingly violates a law which has been properly enacted, if he entertains a religious belief that the law is wrong.[18]

The opinion for the unanimous Court,[19] which included Clifford, Bradley, Harlan, Miller, and Field, was written by Mr. Chief Justice Waite and sustained the validity of the statute as applied. The primary line of reasoning was that the history behind the relevant constitutional principle demonstrated that

"Congress was deprived of all legislative power over mere opinion, but was left free to reach actions which were in violation of social duties or subversive of good order."[20] This proposed distinction between belief and action has often been repeated since, but it is obviously not a line that can provide real assistance in resolving these knotty problems. Consider only a statute which forbade preaching or forbade meetings of religious groups: these must certainly be held violative of the first amendment even though they may be directed only at physical acts. The sounder justification of the result is to be found in a later portion of the opinion, framed in terms similar to the classification principle stated at the outset of this paper. But even this was not untainted by the "action-belief" dichotomy:

> In our opinion, the statute immediately under consideration is within the legislative power of Congress. It is constitutional and valid as prescribing a rule of action for all those residing in the Territories, and in places over which the United States has exclusive control. This being so, the only question which remains is, whether those who make polygamy a part of their religion are excepted from the operation of the statute. If they are, then those who do not make polygamy a part of their religious belief may be found guilty and punished, while those who do, must be acquitted and go free.[21]

In short, if the law is within the scope of governmental authority and of general application,[22] it may—indeed probably must—be applied without regard to the religious convictions of those whose acts constitute wilful violations of that law. To permit individuals to be excused from compliance with the law solely on the basis of religious beliefs is to subject others to punishment for failure to subscribe to those same beliefs.

The tone of the Waite opinion indicates the clear antipathy of the Court to the Mormon sect.[23] But the wrong motivation does not rob the decision of its essential soundness.[24] The same cannot be said of later cases dealing with the Mormons.[25]

In *Davis v. Beason*,[26] a challenge was made to the validity of a statute of the Territory of Idaho that made it a prerequisite to the exercise of the franchise that the voter swear an oath:

> [T]hat I have never been convicted of treason, felony or bribery; . . . that I am not a bigamist or polygamist; that I am not *a member of any order, organization or association which teaches, advises, counsels or encourages its members, devotees or any other person to commit the crime of bigamy or polygamy, or any other crime defined by law, as a duty arising or resulting from membership in such order, organization or association, or which practises bigamy, polygamy or plural or celestial marriage as a doctrinal rite of such organization;* that I do not and will not, publicly or privately, or in any manner whatever teach, advise, counsel or encourage any person to

commit the crime of bigamy or polygamy, or any other crime defined by law, either as a religious duty or otherwise . . . .[27]

Davis, a member of the Mormon church, took the oath and was subsequently indicted for conspiracy with persons unknown to pervert the laws of Idaho by taking the oath falsely. He was found guilty and sentenced to a fine of $500 or 250 days in jail. There was no evidence that Davis was a polygamist or was guilty of any other crime. He did not appeal but immediately sought habeas corpus on the ground that the portion of the statute italicized above violated the first amendment and was, therefore, void. After the trial court refused relief, Davis appealed the denial of the writ to the Supreme Court.

In the Supreme Court, Davis asserted that the territory "could not legally prescribe that a man who has never committed any crime should not have the right to register and vote, or hold office, because he belonged to a church organization that holds or teaches bigamy and polygamy as a doctrine of the church, membership in such organization not having been by law made a crime."[28] He urged three grounds, of interest here, in support of this proposition. First, that the law violated his right to "the free exercise of religion."[29] Second, that the fourteenth amendment, presumably applicable to the Territory of Idaho, made the requirement of the oath unconstitutional. Third, that the legislation violated the provisions of article VI, that "No religious test should be required as a qualification to any office of public trust under the United States." It was under this third rubric that the soundest argument was made condemning the statute as violative of the first amendment:

> That this statute requires a religious test is apparent upon its face. The ground of disenfranchisement is membership in an organization which encourages its members to commit bigamy or polygamy *"as a duty resulting from membership,"* or which *practices* bigamy or polygamy, or celestial marriage, *"as a doctrinal rite of such order."* Simple encouragement to commit crime by an organization of which the citizen is a member does not disqualify him from voting, because, by the language of the act, the encouragement must be offered upon the ground of duty, or religious obligation arising from membership in the organization, or the latter must teach the commission of these acts from religious motives, otherwise the exclusion does not operate. And so also the practice must be "as a doctrinal rite," or the member is not excluded. In other words the practice must be as a tenet of faith, sanctified by a religious ceremony; and the language of the statute does not admit of such an interpretation as will disfranchise the members of an organization existing solely for the promotion of crime, however heinous their acts may be, even though the primary and sole object of the organization be to commit murder, theft, arson, rape and other crimes which are *malum in se*; unless their acts are the promptings of duty, or are performed as "doctrinal rites" or religious ceremonies, the

members are not disqualified by this statute from voting or holding office.

...

The object of this legislation was not only to deprive citizens of the elective franchise because of their membership in a religious organization, the Mormon Church, but to confine the exclusion provided for to members of that religious organization.[30]

Mr. Justice Field, writing for a unanimous Court, paid no heed whatsoever to the argument that the statute, both in fact and in law, singled out members of the Mormon Church for disqualification. *Yick Wo v. Hopkins*,[31] urged on the Court by Davis' counsel, was ignored. The due process requirement was similarly treated with silence. Field cavalierly disposed of the defendant's case in a few sentences at the outset of the opinion:

Bigamy and polygamy are crimes by the laws of all civilized and Christian countries. They are crimes by the laws of the United States, and they are crimes by the laws of Idaho. They tend to destroy the purity of the marriage relation, to disturb the peace of families, to degrade woman and to debase man. Few crimes are more pernicious to the best interests of society and receive more general or more deserved punishment. To extend exemption from punishment for such crimes would be to shock the moral judgment of the community. To call their advocacy a tenet of religion is to offend the common sense of mankind. If they are crimes, then to teach, advise and counsel their practice is to aid in their commission, and such teaching and counseling are themselves criminal and proper subjects of punishment, as aiding and abetting crime are in all other cases.[32]

He resorted again to the distinction between belief and action:

With man's relations to his Maker and the obligations he may think they impose, and the manner in which an expression shall be made by him of his belief on those subjects, no interference can be permitted, provided always the laws of society, designed to secure its peace and prosperity, and the morals of its people, are not interfered with. However free the exercise of religion may be, it must be subordinate to the criminal laws of the country, passed with reference to actions regarded by general consent as properly the subject of punitive legislation.[33]

That such a thesis would have sustained outlawry of the mass, that it would have sustained most of the Tudor legislation restricting Catholics and most of the legislation that forced religious dissenters to leave the shores of Europe for haven in the New World, apparently gave concern to no member of the Court. Field concluded his statement on this issue with the proposition that "Crime is not the less odious because sanctioned by what any particular sect may designate as religion."[34]

In short, the Court sustained the conviction by avoiding the problem. It treated the case as though it presented issues no different from those raised in *Reynolds*. The fact that this statute made membership in the Mormon Church without more a basis for punishment, that the alleged crime was adherence to a religious belief, that in fact that statute was applicable only to the Mormons, was ignored by a Court that could find no sympathy for so militant a Christian minority sect that had caused so much turmoil.[35] The analogy to certain non-Christian organizations of the present day cannot be overlooked. The case has lost its validity for reasons not connected with the religious issue. Certainly it is bad under the test of *Gomillion v. Lightfoot*.[36] It is submitted that it is equally impotent under the proper application of the religion clauses of the first amendment.[37]

3

THE APOCRYPHA

There are in the reports of the Supreme Court of the United States a number of cases frequently referred to for propositions relating to the meaning of the religion clauses of the Constitution that, in fact, rest on grounds completely separate and distinct from those clauses. Based on the misinterpretation of these cases, or on the dicta contained therein, or on practices that have never been subjected to judicial test, propositions have been put forth by various clerical organizations and their champions to support the notion that the separation clause is merely an adjunct to the freedom clause, that its function is to effectuate the principle stated in *Church of the Holy Trinity v. United States,* that "this is a Christian nation."[38] It cannot be gainsaid that there is an inconsistency between the practice of government in many matters and the commands of the first amendment. Lord Bryce explained it thus: "Just because these questions have been long since disposed of, and excite no present passion, and perhaps also because the Americans are more practically easy-going than pedantically exact, the National government, and the State governments do give Christianity a species of recognition inconsistent with the view that civil government should be absolutely neutral in religious matters."[39] But it should be made clear that these practices have not been condoned by Supreme Court decisions, except insofar as their judgments have been misconstrued.

1. *Church of the Holy Trinity v. United States.* In the first of these cases, *Church of the Holy Trinity v. United States,*[40] the question for decision arose out of the imposition of a penalty on a religious corporation on the ground that it violated a federal statute making it illegal to make contracts with foreigners for labor to be performed in this country. The church had contracted with an English clergyman to come to the United States to act as rector and pastor of the Church of the Holy Trinity. The pious Mr. Justice Brewer trotted out all the gimmicks about construing legislation in conformity with the

purpose of the legislature and rightly concluded that the function of the statute was to inhibit the importation of manual laborers: "We find, therefore, that the title of the act, the evil which was intended to be remedied, the circumstances surrounding the appeal to Congress, the reports of the committee of each house, all concur in affirming that the intent of Congress was simply to stay the influx of this cheap unskilled labor."[41]

Brewer, the son of a missionary, chose not to rest here, however. "But beyond all these matters no purpose of action against religion can be imputed to any legislation, state or national, because this is a religious people."[42] In support of this proposition he offered instances of the religious adornments to our history from Columbus to the first amendment. Thus were sown the dragon's teeth that have produced a bitter harvest, for included in the historical panorama, apparently with approval, were such matters as the Delaware test oath[43] and Chancellor Kent's opinion in *People v. Ruggles*,[44] sustaining the notion of the illegality of blasphemy. The opinion is of importance primarily because of such unnecessary dicta. It was correct in its statutory construction and equally so in its thesis that legislation could not single out clergymen—either as individuals or a class—for exclusion from the country. It is submitted that it was in error in any implication that clergymen could be the sole exception to a statutory exclusion of immigrants. Any such classification, in terms of religious occupation, favorable or unfavorable, would run athwart the purposes and provisions of the first amendment.

2. *Pierce v. Society of Sisters*. Probably the most abused citation in the construction of the first amendment is the case of *Pierce v. Society of Sisters*.[45] The case raised no church-state issues; the Court decided no church-state issues. Indeed, no reference to the first amendment is made anywhere in the Court's opinion.

In 1922, the State of Oregon, under the initiative provision of its constitution, adopted a statute that, for all relevant purposes, made attendance at public schools within the state compulsory. The statute was challenged, before it was to become effective, by the Society of Sisters, an Oregon corporation that conducted a school teaching secular and religious subjects, *i.e.*, a parochial school, and by Hill Military Academy, an Oregon corporation conducting a school for secular and military education. The challenge took the form of a suit in the United States District Court, to enjoin the enforcement of the statute. The court issued the injunction. A primary reliance of the schools was on such decisions as the *Child Labor Tax Case*[46] and *Coppage v. Kansas*.[47] In short, the primary arguments put forth were in terms of the "substantive due process" cases that have long since been interred along with the notion that the principles of Spencer's *Social Statics* were incorporated in the Constitution. At that time, however, the Court was still enthralled and the opinion by Mr. Justice McReynolds reads accordingly.

The premise is based on *Meyer v. Nebraska*[48] which held unconstitutional a state statute making it illegal to teach any modern language other than English. The *Meyer* case established for the Court the proposition that there could be no interference with the liberty of parents by "forcing [their children] to accept instruction from public teachers only. The child is not the mere creature of the State; those who nurture him and direct his destiny have the right, coupled with the high duty, to recognize and prepare him for additional obligations."[49] But no parents were parties in the *Pierce* litigation and so the Court had to take a broad jump:

> Appellees are corporations and therefore, it is said, they cannot claim for themselves the liberty which the Fourteenth Amendment guarantees. Accepted in the proper sense, this is true. . . . But they have business and property for which they claim protection. These are threatened with destruction through the unwarranted compulsion which appellants are exercising over present and prospective patrons of their schools. And this court has gone very far to protect against loss threatened by such action. *Truax* v. *Raich*, 239 U.S. 33; *Truax* v. *Corrigan*, 257 U.S. 312; *Terrace* v. *Thompson*, 263 U.S. 197.
>
> . . .
>
> . . . Plaintiffs asked protection against arbitrary, unreasonable and unlawful interference with their patrons and the consequent destruction of their business and property. Their interest is clear and immediate . . . .[50]

Thus does *Pierce* rest clearly on protection of the business and property rights of the schools. Insofar as the liberty of the parents was concerned, that liberty was the freedom to choose schools other than public schools for the education of their children. It was a principle as applicable to the military academy as to the parochial school and, in no way, rested on any concept of "freedom of religion."[51]

3. *Cochran v. Board of Education*. The case of *Cochran v. Board of Educ.*[52] is of importance to the doctrine of church and state under the first amendment, but not, as is generally believed, because the Court was called upon to resolve any substantive issue relating to the religion clauses of the first amendment. Although challenge had been made in the state courts of the power to support church schools, that challenge rested entirely on the provisions of the Louisiana constitution. In the Supreme Court the question presented was only whether the utilization of state funds for private uses controvened the mandate of the due process clause of the fourteenth amendment.

On August 17, 1928, petitioners, taxpayers and parents of school children in the parish of Caddo, Louisiana, sought an injunction from the state trial court to prevent defendants from expending state tax funds on the purchase of school books for children attending private and parochial schools. They asserted that the taxes paid by the petitioners were in excess of the moneys to be expended on school books for their own children and would, therefore, be used to buy school books for children attending private and parochial schools. The assertion was that these expenditures would be illegal because:

> the courses of study and the school books prescribed by the private, reli-
> gious and other schools aforesaid not embraced in the public educational
> system of the State of Louisiana, are different from those prescribed and
> used in the free public schools of this State, and the Louisiana State Board
> of Education has no right or authority to prescribe the course of study or
> the school books to be used by the children attending the schools constitut-
> ing no part of the public educational system of the State of Louisiana, and
> petitioners show that there is a large number of such private and sectarian
> or denominational schools in the State of Louisiana where religious in-
> struction is included in the course of study, and many of the school books
> selected, used and required in such schools, are designed and employed
> to aid and promote the religious beliefs, and to foster and encourage the
> principles of faith, and to teach the tenets of the creed, mode of worship,
> and ecclesiastical policy of the respective churches under whose respective
> control the said schools are conducted.[53]

Only one federal judicial question was raised:

> that the expenditure of said public monies as aforesaid for such illegal
> purposes is the taking of your petitioners' property for a private purpose
> without due process of law . . . in violation of . . . the 14th Amendment
> of the Constitution of the United States.[54]

In addition to other claims of violation of the Louisiana constitution, the petitioners had asserted:

> that said Act violates Section 8 of Article IV of the Constitution of Louisi-
> ana in that it authorizes the taking of money from the public treasury for
> the purpose of teaching religion, and is in aid of churches, sects, or de-
> nominations of religion, which is also in violation of Section 4 of Article
> I of the Constitution of Louisiana . . . .[55]

The respondents admitted all the factual allegations, except that they asserted:

> that it is not their intention nor purpose to furnish free, or otherwise, any
> sectarian or denominational text books to the school children of the State
> of Louisiana . . . and that respondents only propose to furnish such
> books to the educable school children of the State attending schools, cur-
> ricula of which have been approved by the State Board of Education of
> Louisiana.[56]

The state also asserted conclusions that it is not likely to repeat today:

> that the private schools of the State of Louisiana thus become and are,
> agencies of the State, aiding in the education of its children and making it
> possible to educate many thousands who would otherwise be deprived of
> educational advantages. . . . That the primary policy of the aforesaid acts

of the legislature is providing free text books for the educable school children of the State, without discrimination as to race, sex, religion or creed, and respondents aver that if any children of the State are denied the privilege of obtaining free school books from the State of Louisiana because of the fact that such children are attending private or sectarian schools, such discrimination would be arbitrary, unjust and illegal, as well as unconstitutional, and incapable of legal enforcement.[57]

The respondents also attacked the standing of the petitioners to maintain their actions.

The trial court picked up the last challenge. It asserted that municipal taxpayers might have standing to challenge the expenditures of their municipality but that state taxpayers lacked standing to enjoin the expenditure of state funds. After lengthy quotation from the *Frothingham* case,[58] the court concluded:

> The rule held to apply in the affairs of the Federal government should apply with equal, if not greater, force in the affairs of a sovereign state. The interest of the relators as patrons of the public schools is too remote, indirect, and indeterminate to enable them to sue to enjoin a state officer from the disposition of state funds.[59]

A petition for a writ of prohibition from the state supreme court was denied on the ground that the petitioners lacked standing to maintain the action. The Supreme Court of Louisiana entertained the appeal from the lower court judgment of dismissal, however, and held that the petitioners had standing to maintain the action, but ruled in favor of the defendants on the merits.[60] The opinion rationalized the expenditure of funds for school books for children attending parochial schools in terms that have been frequently utilized; the benefits conferred were for the school children and not the schools:

> One may scan the acts in vain to ascertain where any money is appropriated for the purchase of school books for the use of any church, private, sectarian, or even public school. The appropriations were made for the specific purpose of purchasing school books for the use of the school children of the state, free of cost to them. It was for their benefit and the resulting benefit to the state that the appropriations were made. True, these children attend some school, public or private, the latter, sectarian or non-sectarian, and that the books are to be furnished to them for their use, free of cost, whichever they attend. The schools, however, are not the beneficiaries of these appropriations. They obtain nothing from them, nor are they relieved of a single obligation, because of them. The school children and the state alone are the beneficiaries. It is also true that the sectarian schools, which some of the children attend, instruct their pupils in religion, and books are used for that purpose, but one may search diligently the acts, though without result, in an effort to find anything to the effect that it is the purpose of the state to furnish religious books for use of such children.

In fact, in view of the prohibitions in the Constitution against the state's doing anything of that description, it would be legally impossible to interpret the statute as calling for any such action on the part of the state . . . .[61]

The answer of the dissent to this proposition was clear and concise: "It does not require any extended reasoning to produce the conviction that to withdraw money from the public treasury for the purpose of purchasing books to be used in sectarian schools is to use such money 'indirectly' if not 'directly' in aid of the church, sect, or religious denomination conducting the schools."[62]

Although the Supreme Court of the United States, in an opinion by Mr. Chief Justice Hughes, quoted the language of the majority set out above,[63] it was not concerned with the separation issue. At that time it was apparently thought to be a substantial question under the due process clause whether the state moneys were expended for "a public purpose." The Court held that this expenditure in accordance with the statute as interpreted by the Louisiana Supreme Court was for such a purpose and therefore valid under the fourteenth amendment: "The legislation does not segregate private schools, or their pupils, as its beneficiaries or attempt to interfere with any matters of exclusively private concern. Its interest is education, broadly; its method, comprehensive. Individual interests are aided only as the common interest is safeguarded."[64]

Of greater interest to the church-state problem than its decision on the merits was the willingness of the Court to accept the standing of the petitioners in the trial court to raise the question of the propriety of this expenditure of state funds. The issue was quite clearly raised in the Supreme Court by the Attorney General of Louisiana, both in a motion to dismiss for want of jurisdiction[65] and again in the brief on the merits.[66] The Supreme Court did not leave the question open, as it had in the *Providence Hospital* case,[67] nor did it expound on the issue. It simply stated the interest of the appellants and proceeded to deal with the substantive issue. It cannot be treated as less than a holding, albeit sub silentio, that the issue of standing as resolved by the state court, satisfied the requirement of standing to maintain the appeal in the Supreme Court of the United States.

4

THE PROBLEM

OF STANDING TO SUE

The factor that frequently keeps problems of church and state from judicial scrutiny is the absence of a party with recognized standing to bring the issues before the federal courts. In each of the earlier cases discussed above where the issue of the application of the religion clauses was raised in a penal action prosecuted by the United States, the defendants clearly had the right to raise the issue by way of defense. Where the right asserted is put forth in an affirmative rather than a defensive manner, the problem of establishing the existence of justiciable controversy is far more difficult. The Court has utilized various techniques in handling the problem, but has contributed only a confusing diversity rather than clear precedent. The *Pierce* and *Cochran* cases are examples of the inexact nature of the Court's solutions. Two other cases are particularly worthy of comment in the context of the standing problem, a problem that will be found recurrent in the cases to be discussed in later sections of this paper.

1. *The Providence Hospital Case.* One way to secure a federal judicial forum, as evidence by *Cochran*, is for the Court to ignore the problem of the presence of a plaintiff with standing to maintain the action. This is exactly what occurred in *Bradfield v. Roberts*,[68] as well. In *Bradfield*, the plaintiff asserted his rights as a taxpayer of the United States and a resident of the District of Columbia. He sued to enjoin expenditure of federal moneys on the ground that such outlay would violate the separation provision. It has since become abundantly clear that the plaintiff had no authority to raise the question as a taxpayer of the national government.[69] It was more doubtful then. But the Court, in a unanimous opinion by Mr. Justice Peckham, passed quickly over the issue of standing:

> Passing the various objections made to the maintenance of this suit on account of an alleged defect of parties, and also in regard to the character in which the complainant sues, merely that of a citizen and taxpayer of

32

the United States and a resident of the District of Columbia, we come to the main question as to the validity of the agreement between the Commissioners of the District and the directors of the hospital, founded upon the appropriation contained in the act of Congress, the contention being that the agreement if carried out would result in an appropriation by Congress of money to a religious society, thereby violating the constitutional provision which forbids Congress from passing any law respecting an establishment of religion. Art. I of the Amendments to Constitution.[70]

The agreement in question was between the United States and the Providence Hospital. It provided that the Government should pay for the erection of an isolation building on the grounds of the hospital and that the building, upon completion, be turned over to the hospital on conditions (1) that two-thirds of the beds be reserved for the use of poor patients sent there by the commissioners of the district, for whom the United States was to pay at the rate of $250 per annum; and (2) that private patients admitted to the isolation building be permitted to retain physicians and nurses of their own choosing.

The Providence Hospital, it was alleged, was "a private eleemosynary corporation . . . composed of members of a monastic order or sisterhood of the Roman Catholic Church, and is conducted under the auspices of said church; that the title to its property is vested in the Sisters of Charity of Emmitsburg, Maryland . . . ."[71] It was contended, therefore, that moneys paid to it pursuant to the contract would be paid in violation of the separation clause. The Court held that even if payments to a religious corporation would be invalid, the corporation in question was not such a corporation.

> [T]he fact that its members, according to the belief of the complainant, are members of a monastic order or sisterhood of the Roman Catholic Church, and the further fact that the hospital is conducted under the auspices of said church, are wholly immaterial, as is also the allegation regarding the title to its property. . . . Whether the individuals who compose the corporation under its charter happen to be all Roman Catholics, or all Methodists, or Presbyterians, or Unitarians, or members of any other religious organization, or of no organization at all, is of not the slightest consequence with reference to the law of its incorporation, nor can the individual beliefs upon religious matters of the various incorporators be inquired into. Nor is it material that the hospital may be conducted under the auspices of the Roman Catholic Church. . . . The meaning of the allegation is that the church exercises great and perhaps controlling influence over the management of the hospital. It must, however, be managed pursuant to the law of its being.[72]

The Court thereupon affirmed the decision of the lower court dismissing the complaint for failure to set forth a cause of action.

The judgment of the Court, as well as its language, complies with the "neutral principle" suggested at the outset of this paper. But it must be recognized that the Court specifically by-passed the question whether religious corporations—presumably those incorporated for religious purposes—should be similarly treated. It would seem, however, that in so far as the United States was purchasing services or accommodations from private sources, the seller can not be disqualified—any more than it can be qualified—on the ground of religious beliefs. If it were shown that the effect of these services through sectarian facilities in fact resulted in persuasion of the beneficiaries toward the adoption or retention of the Catholic faith, or if it were shown that influences, subtle or direct, were exerted to these ends, or if it were shown that the moneys paid substantially exceeded the value of the services rendered, a different result would be required. Proof of these facts might be difficult, though no more difficult than for those asserted in the *School Segregation* cases.[73] But the allegations of the *Bradfield* complaint, or the fact that the recipient of the moneys from the United States was a sectarian organization, should not suffice to invalidate the contract, whether it be a contract for services or for tangible goods. And this was the conclusion reached by the Court in sustaining the payment by the United States of trust funds to Catholic schools voluntarily attended by Indian beneficiaries of the trust.[74]

2. *Bible Reading.* Some states prohibit Bible reading in the public schools; others command it. Either position arouses the ire of some of the citizens and parents of the community. There are large numbers of state court decisions on the subject, but no one has yet been able to get a full-scale opinion from the Supreme Court of the United States. The Court did decide, in *Washington ex rel. Clithero v. Showalter*,[75] that a state constitutional provision banning Bible reading presented no substantial federal question. But the life of a Supreme Court memorandum decision in this area is very short indeed, and efforts to get the Court to rule on the validity of compulsory Bible reading have failed for one procedural reason or another.

In *Doremus v. Board of Educ.*,[76] two plaintiffs sought a declaratory judgment from the New Jersey courts that a state statute requiring the reading of five verses from the Old Testament at the commencement of each public school day was in violation of the separation requirement of the national constitution. One of the plaintiffs claimed the right to an adjudication on the ground that he was a citizen and taxpayer; the other, in addition to having these attributes, was the parent of a child attending a New Jersey school in which the requirement was in effect. The New Jersey Supreme Court expressed grave doubts about the standing of the plaintiffs to raise the constitutional issue, but avoided decision on the question by ruling against them on the merits.[77]

The Supreme Court, in an opinion by Mr. Justice Jackson, dismissed the appeal for want of a "case or controversy" because of the lack of standing of plaintiffs to maintain the action. The reference to the constitutional standard is of significance in so far as any possibility of statutory cure may be concerned. But the opinion is sufficiently ambiguous, as are the other authorities, to leave the problem in the category of the unresolved.

Jackson said that the plaintiffs could secure no standing by reason of the fact that they were taxpayers. But the language of the opinion leaves unclear the specification of the deficiency, *i.e.*, whether the state taxpayers will be considered in the same way as are national taxpayers under the *Frothingham v. Mellon*[78] doctrine, or whether the defect was in the lack of detail in the plaintiffs' pleading:

> There is no allegation that this activity is supported by any separate tax or paid for from any particular appropriation or that it adds any sum whatever to the cost of conducting the school. No information is given as to what kind of taxes are paid by appellants and there is no averment that the Bible reading increases any tax they do pay or that as taxpayers they are, will, or possibly can be out of pocket because of it.[79]

He distinguished the *Everson*[80] case because "Everson showed a measurable appropriation or disbursement of school-district funds occasioned solely by the activities complained of."[81] The status of parent, which formed the basis for jurisdiction in *McCollum* and *Zorach*,[82] and incidentally in *Showalter*, had been dissipated in this case by the graduation of the child whose parent had brought this suit.

Mr. Justice Douglas dissented, joined by Justices Reed and Burton. They would have held that so long as the New Jersey courts entertained the issue, the Supreme Court should also review it. But the opinion referred to no authority in support of its position.

Neither the majority nor the minority concerned themselves with precedents. No mention was made of *Bradfield v. Roberts*[83] in which the Court specifically by-passed the question but decided the case on the merits, much as the New Jersey court did in *Doremus*. Nor was mention made of *Cochran v. Board of Educ.*[84] or *Heim v. McCall*,[85] where the Court clearly accepted jurisdiction, apparently on the ground that the issue of standing had been resolved by the state court in each case. Nor was any consideration given to *In re Summers*,[86] where the Court found the existence of a case or controversy although the Illinois Supreme Court had ruled that none existed.

The problem is a serious and difficult one. If the state court decision as to standing is not binding on the Supreme Court, the result may be, as in *Doremus*, that a claim of infringement of first amendment rights will have been authoritatively denied by the state court without the possibility of review in the Supreme Court. If the state court determination is binding, the Court may be called on to resolve cases beyond its jurisdiction or to reject cases, as would have been true in *Summers*, because of the state court's refusal to accord standing.

When the Bible-reading controversy was again brought to the Supreme Court, the Court was able to return the case to the three-judge federal court without passing on the question because Pennsylvania had amended its statute in the interim.[87] Thus, both the Bible-reading question and the standing question still remain open for future resolution.

5

"PATRIOTISM IS NOT ENOUGH"

– OR IS IT?

1. *The Selective Draft Law Cases.* The 1917 draft law provided for exemption from service of ministers and students in divinity or theological schools. It also provided that:

> [N]othing in this Act contained shall be construed to require or compel any person to serve in any of the forces herein provided for who is found to be a member of any well-recognized religious sect or organization at present organized and existing and whose existing creed or principles forbid its members to participate in war in any form and whose religious convictions are against war or participation therein in accordance with the creed or principles of said religious organizations . . . .[88]

Here was a classification solely in terms of religion. Those who held certain beliefs and belonged to church organizations appropriate to those beliefs were exempted from duty of military service because of those beliefs and associations. One might have thought that, in a proper case, this would have presented the Court with a serious problem of compliance with the first amendment. It did not. Perhaps because the case in which it was presented was not an appropriate case.

The *Selective Draft Law Cases*[89] brought to the Court appeals from convictions for evasion of the draft law. Among the many issues raised by the defendants was the question whether the classification contained in the language quoted from the statute was invalid as a violation of the first amendment separation clause. Mr. Chief Justice White's opinion for a unanimous Court, rendered during the height of the American participation in World War I, disposed of the issue quickly, but without authority or reason. "And we pass without anything but statement the proposition that an establishment of a religion or an interference with the free exercise thereof repugnant to the First Amendment resulted from the exemption clauses of the act to which we at the outset referred, because we think its unsoundness is too apparent to require us to do more."[90] The decision is as sound as the reasons given for it. The statute did not exempt all whose consciences forbade them to fight. It exempted only those with proper religious allegiances. It may be more difficult for some than it was for Chief Justice White to see why this classification was not a breach in the high wall of separation. It may well be, however, that even if the exemption clause were invalid, the defendants should not have been entitled to relief from prosecution. But that question was never discussed either by the Court or by the Government in its briefs.

2. *Hamilton v. Regents.* In 1931 when pacifism in this country and elsewhere was attaining new converts at a rapid rate, the Southern California Conference of the Methodist Episcopal Church adopted a resolution "to petition the United States Government to grant exemption from military service to such citizens who are members of the Methodist Episcopal Church, as conscientiously believe that participation in war is a denial of their supreme allegiance to Jesus Christ."[91] In 1932, the General Conference of that church petitioned:

> the government of the United States to grant to members of the Methodist Episcopal Church who may be conscientious objectors to war the same exemption from military service as has long been granted to members of the Society of Friends and other similar religious organizations. Similarly we petition all educational institutions which require military training to excuse from such training any student belonging to the Methodist Episcopal Church who has conscientious scruples against it. We earnestly petition the government of the United States to cease to support financially all military training in civil educational institutions.[92]

A similar request to exempt students from military training[93] was presented to the University of California at Berkeley and Los Angeles and to the University of Arizona by the Southern California Conference in 1933. These requests went unheeded. And when Albert W. Hamilton and W. Alonzo Reynolds, Jr., students at U.C.L.A., in turn, requested to be relieved of military training as members of the Methodist Episcopal Church who had conscientious scruples against such service, they too met with failure. When they absented themselves from their R.O.T.C. classes, the University suspended them. The students went directly to the California Supreme Court for relief, seeking a writ of mandamus to compel the University to readmit them without requiring them to attend classes in military training.

The California Supreme Court first rejected the petition without opinion. On rehearing, the unanimous court ruled that the provisions of the organic act creating the University, as well as the regulations of the board of regents, required military training, and that such requirement did not violate any "rights assured to the petitioners by the Constitution of the United States."[94] For this last proposition the California court relied on the judgment of the

Supreme Court holding that the same issue brought up on appeal from a Maryland judgment did not present any substantial federal question.[95]

In the Maryland case,[96] the high court of the state relied upon dicta of the Supreme Court in *United States v. Macintosh*[97] and *Jacobson v. Massachusetts*.[98] The Supreme Court in dismissing for want of a substantial federal question cited several cases to the effect that an appeal may be dismissed where the federal question raised "is wholly formal, is so absolutely devoid of merit as to be frivolous, or has been so explicitly foreclosed by a decision or decisions of this court as to leave no room for real controversy."[99] The citations relevant to the merits spelled out somewhat tenuously the Court's meaning. *Atkin v. Kansas*[100] had held that a state in contracting for public work could impose the condition of a maximum eight-hour day for the employees on the job.

> It cannot be deemed a part of the liberty of any contractor that *he* be allowed to do public work in any mode he may choose to adopt, without regard to the wishes of the State. On the contrary, it belongs to the State, as the guardian and trustee for its people, and having control of its affairs, to prescribe the conditions upon which it will permit public work to be done on its behalf, or on behalf of its municipalities. No court has authority to review its action in that respect. Regulations on this subject suggest only considerations of public policy. And with such considerations the courts have no concern.[101]

The Court seemed to be saying that the conditions on which the state would admit students to its university were entirely at the discretion of the state, including the discretion to demand military training as part of the course of those in attendance. *Heim v. McCall*[102] had reached the same conclusion with regard to a New York requirement that all work on public projects be performed by citizens of the United States. That case had another aspect of interest to church-state issues.[103] *Stephenson v. Binford*[104] similarly had sustained the right of the state to set down conditions on which its highway may be used by a carrier. *Waugh v. Trustees of Univ. of Mississippi*[105] was much closer to the particular issue of attendance at a state university in upholding the state's right to condition a student's admission to its university on his agreement not to become a member of a fraternity. The last of the citations was to the *Macintosh* case, already referred to. The Court appears to have ruled that the question of requiring military training as a condition of attendance at the state university was controlled by these decisions, thus making the question presented an insubstantial one.

It might be regarded as somewhat surprising then, that less than a year after the dismissal of the Maryland case for want of a substantial federal question, the Court should accept jurisdiction in the *Hamilton* case stating that "we are unable to say that every question that appellants have brought here for decision is so clearly not debatable and utterly lacking in merit as to require dismissal for want of substance."[106] On the merits, the Court utilized exactly the arguments of the Maryland court by reference to the *Macintosh* and *Jacobson* cases and then unabashedly noted that the Maryland case, "similar to that now before us, decided against the contention of a student in the University of Maryland who on conscientious grounds objected to military training there required. His appeal to this Court was dismissed for the want of a substantial federal question."[107] This process of turning insubstantial questions into substantial ones and back again in very short periods of time is not an infrequent phenómenon in the area of state-church problems.

More interesting than the majority opinion was that by Mr. Justice Cardozo, joined by Justices Brandeis and Stone. It made explicit the assumption that the religion clauses of the first amendment are incorporated in the fourteenth. But it held, nonetheless, that no infringement of the religion clauses could be found in the circumstances presented. There was no establishment of religion involved, nor was the required instruction "an interference by the state with the free exercise of religion when the liberties of the constitution are read in the light of a century and a half of history during days of peace and war."[108] If the major appeal was to history, a minor one was to practicality:

> Manifestly a different doctrine would carry us to lengths that have never yet been dreamed of. The conscientious objector, if his liberties were to be thus extended, might refuse to contribute taxes in furtherance of a war, whether for attack or for defense, or in furtherance of any other end condemned by his conscience as irreligious or immoral. The right of private judgment has never yet been so exalted above the powers and the compulsion of the agencies of government. One who is a martyr to a principle —which may turn out in the end to be a delusion or an error—does not prove by his martyrdom that he has kept within the law.[109]

The judgment in *Hamilton* is clearly the correct one. Its rationale would seem to have been elliptically spelled out in the citations to the *per curiam* dismissal of the Maryland case for want of a substantial federal question: the issue whether exemption for conscientious beliefs should or should not be granted is one within the discretion of the state legislatures so long as it is equally applied to all. The one thing that the state legislature ought not to be permitted to do was exactly what the students in these cases demanded: to make exemption turn on religious belief or religious affiliation. Were it not for the *Selective Draft Act* cases, it should be clear that exemption from military obligations in terms of religious affiliation is unconstitutional. If military service be considered a duty of every qualified citizen, exemption grants a benefit to religious adherents because they are religious adherents, a result banned by the separation clause. There should be little doubt, for example, that the Government could not refuse commissions in the military service to all members of specified religious sects. It can no more grant benefits on that ground than it can deny them, unless the wall of separation is again to be breached. Cardozo's reference to *Davis v. Beason*[110] suggested that the high wall was to be maintained.

3. *The Flag Salute Cases.* In the flag-salute cases, the thesis for which this paper contends was approximated as it had been in *Reynolds.*[111] Although it prevailed in the first flag-salute opinion, *Minersville School Dist. v. Gobitis,*[112] it was ignored in the opinion overruling the *Gobitis* case, where it became unnecessary to the resolution of the controversy. In *Gobitis*, Mr. Justice Frankfurter, speaking for the Court, said:

> In the judicial enforcement of religious freedom we are concerned with a historic concept. See Mr. Justice Cardozo in *Hamilton* v. *Regents*. . . . The religious liberty which the Constitution protects has never excluded legislation of general scope not directed against doctrinal loyalties of particular sects. Judicial nullification of legislation cannot be justified by attributing to the framers of the Bill of Rights views for which there is no historic warrant. Conscientious scruples have not, in the course of the long struggle for religious toleration, relieved the individual from obedience to a general law not aimed at the promotion or restriction of religious beliefs. The mere possession of religious convictions which contradict the relevant concerns of a political society does not relieve the citizen from the discharge of political responsibilities. The necessity for this adjustment has again and again been recognized. In a number of situations the exertion of political authority has been sustained, while basic considerations of religious freedom have been left inviolate. . . . In all these cases the general laws in question, upheld in their application to those who refused obedience from religious conviction, were manifestations of specific powers of government deemed by the legislature essential to secure and maintain that orderly, tranquil, and free society without which religious toleration itself is unattainable.[113]

The argument as thus presented failed to take into consideration, in its support, the relevance of the separation clause. That gap was to be filled in the subsequent dissent from the judgment overruling *Gobitis*. For it is necessarily true that to exempt from duties and burdens on the ground of religious belief is to afford a benefit to those exempted on that ground.

If the *Gobitis* case was not the last neither was it the first in a series of Supreme Court rulings on the validity of compulsory flag-salute laws. Legislation requiring participation in flag-salute ceremonies at public schools was widespread. It was frequently challenged. The flag-salute statutes of Georgia, New Jersey, Massachusetts, California, and New York were all sustained. All but the last were brought to the Supreme Court for consideration. In the cases of the Georgia and New Jersey legislation, the Court dismissed appeals for want of a substantial federal question,[114] relying primarily on *Hamilton v. Regents*. The Massachusetts statute was sustained by a three-judge federal court, whose judgment was affirmed without opinion by the Supreme Court.[115] Certiorari was denied in the California case.[116] No review was sought of the New York judgment.[117] Despite this plethora of authority, the Court of Appeals for the Third Circuit sustained the judgment of a trial court that the Pennsylvania flag-salute requirement was unconstitutional.[118] It was this judgment that the Court reviewed in the *Gobitis* case.

The legislation in question in *Gobitis* was a school regulation of the Board of Education of the Minersville Public Schools:

> That the Superintendent of the Minersville Public Schools be required to demand that all teachers and pupils of said schools be required to salute the flag of our country as part of the daily exercises. That refusal to salute the flag shall be regarded as an act of insubordination and shall be dealt with accordingly.[119]

Lillian and William Gobitis, aged twelve and ten respectively, refused to participate in the flag-salute ceremonies, and were expelled from school. Because of the compulsory education laws their father was compelled to send them to private schools or risk the penalty for the children's delinquency. He brought suit in the Pennsylvania courts on his own behalf and that of the children to compel reinstatement. The complaint alleged, inter alia, that their exclusion was in violation of their freedom of religious belief because the tenets of their faith regarded the flag salute as contradictory to the command of their religion specified in verses 4 and 5 of chapter 20 of *Exodus:* "Thou shalt not make unto thee any graven image, or any likeness of any thing that is in heaven above, or that is in the earth beneath, or that is in the water under the earth; Thou shalt not bow down thyself to them, nor serve them . . . ."[120]

Judge Maris, then sitting in the district court, granted the relief requested. He distinguished the *Hamilton* case:

> In the case before us the attendance of the minor plaintiffs at defendants' schools is, as we have seen, required by law. Furthermore their refusal to salute the flag does not prejudice the public safety. Consequently Hamilton . . . does not support the validity of the regulation here involved. On the contrary that regulation, although undoubtedly adopted from patriotic motives, appears to have become in this case a means for the persecution of children for conscience' sake. Our beloved flag, the emblem of religious liberty, apparently has been used as an instrument to impose a religious test as a condition of receiving the benefits of public education. And this has been done without any compelling necessity of public safety or welfare. . . . In these days when religious intolerance is again rearing its ugly head in other parts of the world it is of the utmost importance that the lib-

erties guaranteed to our citizens by the fundamental law be preserved from all encroachment.[121]

He also found: "The enforcement of defendants' regulation requiring the flag salute by children who are sincerely opposed to it upon conscientious religious grounds is not a reasonable method of teaching civics, including loyalty to the State and Federal Government, but tends to have the contrary effect upon such children."[122]

Judge Clark of the Third Circuit wrote an opinion affirming the judgment.[123] In essence, he ruled that in a conflict between religious belief and state interests, the latter must bow:

> To summarize our analysis: compulsory flag saluting is designed to better secure the state by inculcating in its youthful citizens a love of country that will incline their hearts and minds to its more willing defense. That particular compulsion happens to be abhorrent to the particular love of God of the little girl and boy now seeking our protection. One conception or the other must yield. Which is required by our Constitution? We think the material and not the spiritual.[124]

The School Board's argument that the flag salute was not a religious ceremony,[125] like the Gobitis' argument that the word of the Bible was superior to the Constitution,[126] was disregarded by the Court as inappropriate to the issue before it. It remained for the amici curiae to deal with the underlying issue: was it within the power of the State of Pennsylvania, the issue of religious liberty aside, to compel the salute of the flag? The American Civil Liberties Union brief, set down two *ipse dixits*. The first: "The salute prescribed by the Minersville Board of Education is not—like military service and preparation to render it—a practice which Government may encourage by rewards and punishments, but is a ceremony having no value except as a voluntary expression of sentiment and belief."[127] Second: "It is not competent for Pennsylvania to involve the flag of the United States in a controversy with its citizens over the forms of respect which loyalty to the flag and Government of the United States demand."[128] The amicus brief filed by a committee of the American Bar Association asserted:

> The requirement of such a ritual is clearly alien to our institutions. It would be an intolerable invasion of individual liberties. Because it is inherent in the very nature of Americans to resent unnecessary assertions of authority, such a measure would not further the end of promoting loyalty and strengthening morale, but would have precisely the opposite effect. It would be unconstitutional because there would be no 'appropriate relation' between the legislative command and the prescribed punishment, on the one hand, and the avowed objective on the other.[129]

This issue the Court met head on: "The wisdom of training children in patriotic impulses by those compulsions which necessarily pervade so much of the educational process is not for our independent judgment. Even were we convinced of the folly of such a measure, such belief would be no proof of its unconstitutionality."[130] Once that premise was established, the principle quoted at the beginning of this section compelled the conclusion that there could be no release from the duty solely on religious grounds.

Mr. Justice Stone's dissent rested in part on a lack of belief in the validity of the compulsion. He talked of "a supposed educational measure."[131] Because the compulsory flag salute is of such doubtful value in inculcating patriotism, the State's demands might be modified by the competing interests of freedom. Throughout his opinion there were suggestions that freedom of speech was as much at issue as freedom of religion. But it was on religion that he ultimately rested: "And while such expressions of loyalty, when voluntarily given, may promote national unity, it is quite another matter to say that their compulsory expression by children in violation of their own and their parents' religious convictions can be regarded as playing so important a part in our national unity as to leave school boards free to exact it despite the constitutional guarantee of freedom of religion."[132] Because in his mind the Court was free to indulge in balancing the benefits to the State against the harm to religious freedom, he did not answer the question whether a student could constitutionally be compelled to salute the flag if his objections to doing so were based on other than religious grounds. If he would treat the two cases differently he would have had to deal with the separation clause. If he would treat the two similarly then his conclusion could not have rested on the proposition of religious freedom.

It is not often that a Court, divided eight to one, will reverse itself within a period of three years. But the *Gobitis* case was specifically overruled within such a period by *Board of Educ. v. Barnette.*[133] There had been a change of personnel in the interim. Stone had succeeded Hughes as Chief Justice; McReynolds had retired; Jackson and Rutledge had been appointed. But the new justices did not themselves account for the difference: Black, Douglas, and Murphy shifted their positions in the interim.

The opinion by Mr. Justice Jackson for the Court stated the question to include the problem whether the requirement may be imposed on those whose objections rested on other than religious grounds. In doing so, he was a bit disingenuous about what the Court had done in the earlier case:

> Nor does the issue as we see it turn on one's possession of particular religious views or the sincerity with which they are held. While religion supplies appellees' motive for enduring the discomforts of making the issue in this case, many citizens who do not share these religious views hold such a compulsory rite to infringe constitutional liberty of the individual. It is

not necessary to inquire whether non-conformist beliefs will exempt from the duty to salute unless we first find power to make the salute a legal duty.

The *Gobitis* decision, however, *assumed*, as did the argument in that case and in this, that power exists in the State to impose the flag salute discipline upon school children in general. The Court only examined and rejected a claim based on religious beliefs of immunity from an unquestioned general rule. The question which underlies the flag salute controversy is whether such a ceremony so touching matters of opinion and political attitude may be imposed upon the individual by official authority under powers committed to any political organization under our Constitution.[134]

In short, the question to be examined, in fact put in the *Barnette* case and answered by the majority in the negative,[135] was whether any child, regardless of religious belief could be compelled to engage in the rite of the flag salute. The difference between the two judgments was not in the question but in the answer: "We think the action of the local authorities in compelling the flag salute and pledge transcends constitutional limitations on their power and invades the sphere of intellect and spirit which it is the purpose of the First Amendment to our Constitution to reserve from all official control."[136] The difference between the opinions of the Court in *Barnette* and *Gobitis* rested on the answer to the question whether the compulsion could be exerted as to anyone, not on the answer to the question whether the religious freedom clause exempted those asserting religious beliefs from obligations that could be imposed on all who do not assert such beliefs.

Justices Black and Douglas, however, preferred the proposition "that the statute before us fails to accord full scope to the freedom of religion secured to the appellees by the First and Fourteenth Amendments."[137] They followed the Stone position in *Gobitis*, although Stone himself joined the Jackson opinion. They would now test imposition on religious freedom in terms of the existence of "a grave danger" to the community resulting from failure to comply with the commands of the state. This thesis, of course, would leave the States free to continue the compulsory flag salute with reference to all who do not, because of their religion, construe the words of *Exodus* as a higher command than that of the State; a command not to salute the flag. Mr. Justice Murphy joined the Jackson opinion, but added one of his own. Although the doctrine to be found there is difficult to refine, it would appear that he rested both on the proposition offered by Mr. Justice Jackson and that offered by Justices Black and Douglas.

Mr. Justice Frankfurter's dissenting opinion dealt with both propositions. He rejected Jackson's argument that the flag salute was an invalid means to a legitimate end: the Court's evaluation of the validity of the means was necessarily to be subordinated to that of the legislature. Whether the flag salute is a means of inculcating a spirit of patriotism and loyalty is sufficiently debatable to require the subordination of the judicial assessment to the legislative judgment. Of more interest here is the answer to those who would grant special exemption—because of religious doctrine—from a requirement that may be imposed on others. Excerpts cannot give the flavor of this opinion, but they can reveal the guiding principle. If the opinion proved unconvincing to other members of the Court, it apparently also proved unanswerable. The majority need not have responded to it because the asserted principle was not in conflict with the majority opinion; the minority chose not to respond to it, although each of them, except the Chief Justice, had once adhered to it.

> The constitutional protection of religious freedom terminated disabilities, it did not create new privileges. It gave religious equality, not civil immunity. Its essence is freedom from conformity to religious dogma, not freedom from conformity to law because of religious dogma. Religious loyalties may be exercised without hindrance from the state, not the state may not exercise that which except by leave of religious loyalties is within the domain of temporal power. Otherwise each individual could set up his own censor against obedience to laws conscientiously deemed for the public good by those whose business it is to make laws.[138]
>
> The essence of the religious freedom guaranteed by our Constitution is therefore this: no religion shall either receive the state's support or incur its hostility. Religion is outside the sphere of political government. This does not mean that all matters on which religious organizations or beliefs may pronounce are outside the sphere of government. Were this so, instead of the separation of church and state, there would be the subordination of the state on any matter deemed within the sovereignty of the religious conscience. Much that is the concern of temporal authority affects the spiritual interests of men. But it is not enough to strike down a nondiscriminatory law that it may hurt or offend some dissident view. It would be too easy to cite numerous prohibitions and injunctions to which laws run counter if the variant interpretations of the Bible were made the tests of obedience to law. The validity of secular laws cannot be measured by their conformity to religious doctrines. It is only in a theocratic state that ecclesiastical doctrines measure legal right or wrong.[139]
>
> Certainly this Court cannot be called upon to determine what claims of conscience should be recognized and what should be rejected as satisfying the "religion" which the Constitution protects. That would indeed resurrect the very discriminatory treatment of religion which the Constitution sought forever to forbid.[140]

The flag-salute cases left the law clear on the question whether the states may compel that ceremony.[141] Inasmuch as the majority opinion in the *Barnette* case did not rest on the religious freedom ground for decision, it left unrefined the principles applicable to that portion of the first amendment. The cases clearly left a conflict between the principles enunciated by two minority opinions, that of Justices Black and Douglas and that of Mr. Justice Frankfurter. It is not helpful to prognosis that of all the Justices who sat on the *Barnette* case, these three alone are still participating in the work of the Court.[142]

4. *Conscientious Objection and Admission to the Bar*. The connection between conscientious objection to military service and the obligation to perform military duties or train for military service is patent. Somewhat less clear, perhaps, is the nexus between an undertaking to bear arms and one's right to citizenship. Almost elusive, however, is the relationship between conscientious objection to military duty and the capacity to practice law. Illinois thought that there was sufficient connection to preclude a conscientious objector from admission to its bar. And the Supreme Court was able to discern the reasonableness of that position, or at least the absence of unreasonableness, in *In re Summers*.[143]

Summers was a graduate of the University of Illinois Law School. He had been classified as a conscientious objector relieved of military service by his draft board; for physical reasons he had not been called upon to do non-combatant service. He had passed the bar examinations and was teaching law at the University of Toledo at the time of his application for admission. He was refused admission to the bar by the character and fitness committee whose judgment was sustained by the Illinois Supreme Court. The Supreme Court of Illinois announced that he was rejected "because he is a conscientious objector."[144]

At the hearings before the character and fitness committee, the record of which presents a rather sorry spectacle,[145] it developed that Summers was a conscientious objector because of his belief in Gandhi's principles of passive resistance, principles that he also derived from the teachings of the New Testament. He did not assert that his refusal to perform military duty was because of his religion: he was a Methodist. Indeed, throughout the hearings he drew a distinction between his position as a "conscientious" objector and the position of others who were "religious" objectors.[146] But when the case came to the Supreme Court one of the primary grounds for attack was the violation of the petitioner's freedom of religion.

The opinion of the Court, written by Mr. Justice Reed, after disposing of the question of jurisdiction,[147] quickly concluded that the State of Illinois had not violated the national constitution in preventing Summers' admission to the bar. In reaching his conclusion, he erroneously relied on the cases in which the United States had denied naturalization to would-be citizens who refused to take an oath to defend the country by taking up arms in time of war:

> It is impossible for us to conclude that the insistence of Illinois that an officer who is charged with the administration of justice must take an oath to support the Constitution of Illinois and Illinois' interpretation of

that oath to require a willingness to perform military service violates the principles of religious freedom which the Fourteenth Amendment secures against state action, when a like interpretation of a similar oath as to the Federal Constitution bars an alien from national citizenship.[148]

The fact is that neither *Schwimmer*[149] nor *Macintosh*[150] involved a similar constitutional question. Mr. Justice Black in his dissent made a similar erroneous reliance on the dissents in these cases: "Dissents in both cases rested in part on the premise that religious tests are incompatible with our constitutional guarantee of freedom of thought and religion."[151] Mr. Chief Justice Hughes made clear in *Macintosh* what the issue really was in that case and the same issue was presented in *Schwimmer:*

> It is important to note the precise question to be determined. It is solely one of law, as there is no controversy as to the facts. The question is not whether naturalization is a privilege to be granted or withheld. That it is such a privilege is undisputed. Nor, whether the Congress has the power to fix the conditions upon which the privilege is granted. That power is assumed. Nor, whether the Congress may in its discretion compel service in the army in time of war or punish the refusal to serve. That power is not here in dispute. Nor is the question one of the authority of Congress to exact a promise to bear arms as a condition of its grant of naturalization. That authority, for the present purpose, may also be assumed.
>
> The question before the Court is the narrower one whether the Congress has exacted such a promise.[152]

Only if the Court, in *Summers*, was willing to "assume" or treat as "undisputed" the power of Illinois to condition admission to the bar in the same way that Congress conditioned naturalization could it reach the same conclusion. But the very question presented in *Summers* was whether there was constitutional warrant for such powers as were not in contest in *Schwimmer-Macintosh*. In short, the constitutional question was present in *Summers;* it was not present in *Schwimmer-Macintosh*, so that the latter can hardly be authority for the former.

The closer analogy is the flag-salute cases. If the state has the power to compel the flag salute as a condition of remaining in school, it would seem that the religious objection should not permit exemption. But as the majority held in the *Barnette* case, the state has no right to compel such action from any individual. So, too, it would seem that if the state has a constitutional right to compel the oath to bear arms as a condition of admission to the bar, the religious ground for exception ought not to be a basis for relief. The Court in *Summers* found that the power did exist, although there would seem to be less rational connection between the oath and practice of law than between the compulsion to salute and the inculcation of patriotic dedication.

Mr. Justice Black's dissent, for himself and three of his brethren, recognized the relevance of *Barnette*, but would seem to give it different significance. He said: "I cannot agree that a state can lawfully bar from a semi-public position a well-qualified man of good character solely because he entertains a religious belief which might prompt him at some time in the future to violate a law which has not yet been and may never be enacted."[153] The question should have been whether the state could bar that individual whether his belief rested on a religious basis or not. The dissenters' answer would probably have been the same. And if it were it would have been concerned with the facts of this case, when it is recalled that Summers' objections on the record purported to derive from "conscientious" rather than "religious" objection. Then, too, the *Barnette* decision would have been a more relevant guide to decision.

6

THE RIGHT TO PROSELYTE

It is not infrequent that those most intolerant of the rights of others are the most vigorous in seeking the protection of their own. A large part of the constitutional law relating to freedom of religion has been developed because of the readiness of the Jehovah's Witnesses to resort to the courts for the protection of their rights and their ability to sustain the costs of carrying their cases to the Supreme Court. Particularly in that area where freedom of religion blends into freedom of speech have the Witnesses been active, with resulting confusion of doctrine but expansion of the right of militant minority sects to the protection of the state in their virulent attacks on the views of others.

1. *Lovell and Schneider.* The first of the Jehovah's Witness cases to be given full hearing by the Supreme Court was that of Alma Lovell.[154] She was convicted of violating a city ordinance that forbade distribution of handbills or literature on the streets of the metropolis of Griffin, Georgia without first securing a permit from the City Manager. She had failed to apply for a permit to distribute copies of the "Kingdom of Jehovah," because application for such a permit was contrary to her religious beliefs. She contended that the restraint of the ordinance violated her rights to religious freedom, freedom of the press, freedom of speech, and other constitutional guarantees.

Earlier, the same ordinance was attacked on similar facts but solely on the ground that it was violative of freedom of religion. The Court of Appeals of Georgia sustained it against such attack.[155] On appeal to the Supreme Court, the appeal was dismissed for want of a substantial federal question.[156] It was argued in *Lovell* that the earlier decision had disposed of the problem. The Court rejected the argument: "[I]n the *Coleman* case, the Court did not deal with the question of freedom of speech and of the press, as it had not been properly presented."[157] The Court proceeded to hold that the ordinance under

50

attack violated freedom of the press "by subjecting it to license and censorship."[158] In combination, the two cases from Griffin necessarily hold that the protection afforded did not come from the religous freedom clause but rather from the freedom of press clause, and thus the right of distribution was protected for all whether circulating religious pamphlets or other literature.

Similar problems with municipal ordinances requiring licenses for the distribution of literature came to the Court in the 1939 Term, as a result of arrests and convictions of Jehovah's Witnesses.[159] Again the Court acted almost unanimously, as it had in the *Lovell* case, by finding the ordinances in violation of the freedom of speech and press clauses. "To require a censorship through license which makes impossible the free and unhampered distribution of pamphlets strikes at the very heart of the constitutional guarantees."[160] Again the protection afforded was in no way restricted to those distributing religious literature, except that the Court did exempt "commercial soliciting and canvassing" from the protected areas.[161]

2. *Cantwell v. Connecticut.* Freedom of religion was not used to justify the Court's position in the licensing cases until its decision in *Cantwell v. Connecticut*.[162] That case arose out of the arrest of a father and his two minor sons for engaging in the distribution of the literature of their sect and the playing of phonograph records setting out its doctrine. Their practice was to go from door to door and to utilize street corners for their propaganda efforts. They offered to sell the books and pamphlets that they had, but if no purchase was made they offered to leave a pamphlet or book with the prospect on payment of any contribution.[163] The content of the materials that the Cantwells were distributing was typical of the literature of their sect.[164] On the occasion in question, they chose to engage in their calling in a neighborhood ninety per cent of whose residents were members of the Roman Catholic Church.

All three of the defendants were convicted on two of the five counts in the information: the third, which charged violation of a statute prohibiting solicitation without license, and the fifth, alleging breach of the peace, a common-law crime in Connecticut. The statute involved provided:

> No person shall solicit money, services, subscriptions or any valuable thing for any alleged religious, charitable or philanthropic cause, from other than a member of the organization for whose benefit such person is soliciting or within the county in which such person or organization is located unless such cause shall have been approved by the secretary of the public welfare council. Upon application of any person in behalf of such cause the secretary shall determine whether such cause is a religious one or is a bona fide object of charity or philanthropy and conforms to reasonable standards of efficiency and integrity, and, if he shall so find, shall approve the same and issue to the authority in charge a certificate to that effect. Such certificate may be revoked at any time. Any person violating

any provision of this section shall be fined not more than one hundred dollars or imprisoned not more than thirty days or both.[165]

The breach of the peace count charged them with "inciting to violence or tending or provoking' others to break the peace," by playing the records to patently hostile listeners. The defendants asserted throughout the proceedings in the Connecticut courts and in the Supreme Court that their convictions violated their rights of freedom of speech and religion as guaranteed by the fourteenth amendment. The Connecticut Supreme Court of Errors affirmed the conviction of the father on both the third and fifth counts, affirmed the convictions of the sons on the third count, but reversed them on the fifth.[166] In denying the claims of the invalidity of the statutory count, the Connecticut court said:

> The further contention that this statute, as applied to the acts of the defendants, is invalid under . . . the due process clause of the Fourteenth Amendment . . . appears to be based upon a claim that the statute . . . abridges or denies freedom of religious profession and worship and liberty of speech and of the press. . . . § 6294 does not apply, and is not sought to be applied in this case, to the dissemination, either by sale or free distribution, of printed matter by the defendants. . . . [T]he purpose of the statute is to protect the public against imposition in the matter of solicitations of funds purportedly for religious, charitable, or philanthropic causes. This is not, and is not claimed to be, objectionable on constitutional grounds. It is such solicitation which brings defendants within the statute, not their other and apparently predominant activities in the dissemination of literature.[167]

The Connecticut court, in sustaining the conviction under the fifth count only as to the father, narrowed the issues again. "The doing of acts or the use of language which, under circumstances of which the person is or should be aware, are calculated or likely to provoke another person or other persons to acts of immediate violence may constitute a breach of the peace."[168] "It is not necessary, as claimed, to show that other persons were actually provoked to the point of violence or disturbance of the peace."[169]

The issues as thus drawn by the Connecticut court were rather narrow: (1) could the state properly qualify solicitation of funds by the licensing requirement set out in the statute; (2) could the state make it a crime to use speech calculated or likely to provoke a breach of the peace.

Although the Supreme Court was not pellucid in the announcement of the controlling doctrine, there is evidence in the opinion of the application of the proper standard: classification in terms of religion, whether it be for purposes of controlling solicitation of funds or controlling some other conduct is invalid. The Court, speaking through Mr. Justice Roberts put it this way:

The general regulation, in the public interest, of solicitation, which does not involve any religious test and does not unreasonably obstruct or delay the collection of funds, is not open to any constitutional objection, even though the collection be for a religious purpose. Such regulation would not constitute a prohibited previous restraint on the free exercise of religion or interpose an inadmissible obstacle to its exercise.

It will be noted, however, that the Act requires an application to the secretary of the public welfare council of the State; that he is empowered to determine whether the cause is a religious one, and that the issue of a certificate depends upon his affirmative action. If he finds that the cause is not that of religion, to solicit for it becomes a crime. He is not to issue a certificate as a matter of course. His decision to issue or refuse it involves appraisal of the facts, the exercise of judgment, and the formation of an opinion. He is authorized to withhold his approval if he determines that the cause is not a religious one. Such a censorship of religion as the means of determining its right to survive is a denial of liberty protected by the First Amendment and included in the liberty which is within the protection of the Fourteenth.[170]

The Court emphasized the discriminatory nature of the regulation involved and the fact that its deficiencies were in terms of the improper classification:

Nothing we have said is intended even remotely to imply that, under the cloak of religion, persons may, with impunity, commit frauds upon the public. Certainly penal laws are available to punish such conduct. Even the exercise of religion may be at some slight inconvenience in order that the State may protect its citizens from injury. Without doubt a State may protect its citizens from fraudulent solicitations by requiring a stranger in the community, before permitting him publicly to solicit funds for any purpose, to establish his identity and his authority to act for the cause which he purports to represent. The State is likewise free to regulate the time and manner of solication generally, in the interest of public safety, peace, comfort or convenience. But to condition the solicitation of aid for the perpetuation of religious views or systems upon a license, the grant of which rests in the exercise of a determination by state authority as to what is a religious cause, is to lay a forbidden burden upon the exercise of liberty protected by the Constitution.[171]

When dealing with the problem of the conviction for breach of the peace, the Court again resorted to standards and tests applicable to all and did not rest its decision to upset the verdict of guilt on religious freedom but rather on principles of freedom of speech. Although the Court talked of two "liberties," undefined except in terms of "the realm of religious faith, and in that of political belief,"[172] the equation of the two, and the utilization of *Schenck, Herndon v. Lowry,* and *Thornhill,*[173] as authority suggested that the protection flowed from principles not derived from the religion clauses of the first amendment:

> Although the contents of the record not unnaturally aroused animosity, we think that, in the absence of a statute narrowly drawn to define and punish specific conduct as constituting a clear and present danger to a substantial interest of the State, the petitioner's communication, considered in the light of the constitutional guarantees, raised no such clear and present menace to public peace and order as to render him liable to conviction of the common law offense in question.[174]

It cannot be suggested that the doctrine put forth at the outset of this article was specifically adopted by the Court in the *Cantwell* case. But it is clear that the results reached there and the language used are consistent with the proposed method for handling these problems. The holding was a narrow one precluding the State from the exercise of its licensing power on the basis of its determination of "what is a religious cause." The holding should be distinguished from the gloss later put on *Cantwell* so that it has become much more than it was.

3. *Cox, Chaplinsky, Jamison, and Largent.* In *Cox v. New Hampshire*,[175] the Court dealt summarily with a claim that a State statute requiring a license for a parade and a fee for the license was invalid as applied to processions of Jehovah's Witnesses walking in close order on the streets of Manchester for the purpose of advertising, primarily by placards, a meeting at which the dogma of the sect would be preached. The convictions for the violation of the statute were attacked under both the free speech provision and the freedom of religion clause of the first amendment. The unanimous Court, speaking through Mr. Chief Justice Hughes, found no infringement of the rights of speech. The statute was a valid means of controlling the use of the streets. "There is no evidence that the statute has been administered otherwise than in the fair and non-discriminatory manner which the state court has construed it to require."[176]

The Court distinguished the *Cantwell* case on the ground that the statute there "authorized an official to determine whether the cause was a religious one and to refuse a permit if he determined that it was not, thus establishing a censorship of religion."[177] The freedom of religion argument just sank of its own weight. "No interference with religious worship or the practice of religion in any proper sense is shown, but only the exercise of local control over the use of streets for parades and processions."[178] The religious element properly provided no basis for distinguishing the treatment of the defendants here from any defendants parading in a non-religious cause or no cause at all.

Chaplinsky v. New Hampshire[179] brought a question closer to the second issue of the *Cantwell* case. Chaplinsky was convicted for violation of a New Hampshire statute that made it a crime to "address any offensive, derisive or annoying word to any other person who is lawfully in any street or other public place, [or to] call him by any offensive or derisive name, [or to] make any noise or exclamation in his presence and hearing with intent to deride, offend or annoy him, or to prevent him from pursuing his lawful business or occupation."[180] He had been engaged in distributing literature of the type involved in *Cantwell* on the streets of Rochester on Saturday afternoon. The city marshal received complaints about his language but informed the complainants that Chaplinsky was "lawfully engaged." He then warned Chaplinsky that the crowd was getting restless. Later, a disturbance occurred and a police officer took Chaplinsky into custody and started him on the way to the police station. They passed the marshal who was on the way to the scene of the disturbance where, he had been informed, a riot was under way. It was at this time that Chaplinsky, apparently in retort to remarks of the marshal, called the marshal a "damned racketeer" and "a damned Fascist" and said that "the whole government of Rochester are Fascists or agents of Fascists."[181] It was for the use of this language that he was prosecuted and convicted.

The Court again unanimously affirmed the conviction. This time the opinion was written by Mr. Justice Murphy. The religion issue was quickly put to one side:

> [W]e cannot conceive that cursing a public officer is the exercise of religion in any sense of the term. But even if the activities of the appellant which preceded the incident could be viewed as religious in character, and therefore entitled to the protection of the Fourteenth Amendment, they would not cloak him with immunity from the legal consequences for concomitant acts committed in violation of a valid criminal statute.[182]

It is hard to tell what the Court is saying at this point, assuming that it is not defining what is and what is not religion. But its action is clear. It treated the defendant here as it would any defendant not offering the cloak of religion for immunity. The doctrines of freedom of speech do not protect the utterances in question.[183] The conviction must therefore be sustained.

Jamison v. Texas[184] was another case involving a municipal ordinance similar to those successfully attacked and held invalid in *Lovell* and *Schneider* on the ground of improper infringement of the rights of free speech and press. The *Jamison* case could have rested on these grounds alone. It probably did. But the language chosen by the Court, in an opinion by Mr. Justice Black, unduly and unfortunately, sowed the seeds for argument that it was the religious element that contributed to downfall of the ordinances in the earlier cases. A simple comparison between the two *Griffin* cases referred to earlier,[185] in which the Court refused to strike down an ordinance on religious freedom grounds alone but did strike down the same ordinance applied to the same activity on freedom of speech and press grounds, demonstrates the unreliability of reading the earlier cases as turning on the religious issue. The unfortunate language, in an opinion written for all the participating justices, was this:

> The right to distribute handbills concerning religious subjects on the streets may not be prohibited at all times, at all places, and under all circumstances. This has been beyond controversy since . . . *Lovell* . . . . The city contends, however, that in the instant case the prohibition is permissible because the handbills, although they were distributed for the unquestioned purpose of furthering religious activity, contained an invitation to contribute to the support of that activity by purchasing books related to the work of the group. The mere presence of an advertisement of a religious work on a handbill of the sort distributed here may not subject the distribution of the handbill to prohibition. In *Schneider* . . . we held that the city of Irvington might not forbid conduct almost precisely the same as that with which the appellant in the instant case is charged. Even where handbills carrying notice of a public gathering contained a statement of an admission fee, we held that they could not be barred from distribution on the streets. . . . No admission was to be charged at the meeting for which the appellant was circulating leaflets in the instant case. In *Cantwell* . . . we said that a state might not prevent the collection of funds for a religious purpose by unreasonably obstructing or delaying their collection.[186]

That this is a distortion of the holding of *Cantwell* is apparent from a reading of that opinion. The essence of the unconstitutionality there was the power given to the authorities to determine what was and what was not a religious cause. Why this unnecessary construction should have been utilized here, with the concurrence of the entire Court, is far from clear. What is clear is that such reconstruction is typical of the way that constitutional law grows or, at least, changes.[187]

Mr. Justice Black went on:

> The states can prohibit the use of the streets for the distribution of purely commercial leaflets, even though such leaflets may have "a civic appeal, or a moral platitude" appended. *Valentine* v. *Chrestensen*, 316 U.S. 52, 55. They may not prohibit the distribution of handbills in the pursuit of a clearly religious activity merely because the handbills invite the purchase of books for the improved understanding of the religion or because the handbills seek in a lawful fashion to promote the raising of funds for religious purposes.[188]

The logical next step was taken by the Court on the same day that it handed down the *Jamison* case. In *Largent v. Texas*,[189] in a unanimous opinion for the Court by Mr. Justice Reed, the protection afforded the distribution of Jehovah's Witness literature, became a matter of religious freedom. The factual data was not different from the earlier cases attacking municipal ordinances requiring permits for the distribution of literature. Mr. Justice Reed, after disposing of a jurisdictional problem, met the constitutional questions this way:

> Upon the merits, this appeal is governed by recent decisions of this Court involving ordinances which leave the granting or withholding of permits for the distribution of religious publications in the discretion of municipal officers. It is unnecessary to determine whether the distributions of the publications in question are sales or contributions. The mayor issues a permit only if after thorough investigation he "deems it proper or advisable." Dissemination of ideas depends upon the approval of the distributor by the official. This is administrative censorship in an extreme form. It abridges the freedom of religion, of the press and of speech guaranteed by the Fourteenth Amendment.[190]

What was appreciated by the earlier judgments but not by those of the 1942 Term was that the unconstitutionality of the restraint turned on the censorship of the dissemination of ideas and not on the religious nature of those ideas. If the censorship were invalid with regard to other literature it was equally invalid with reference to religious literature. If it were valid with reference to other literature, to invalidate it solely with reference to religious literature was to aid religion in violation of the separation clause by affording it protections not given to other writings.

4. *Murdock, Jones, Martin, and Douglas.* The culmination of the movement from the *Griffin* cases, which protected the right to free press and free speech, was *Murdock v. Pennsylvania,*[191] where religious literature was accorded special protection above and beyond the rights of speech and press. The reconstruction of the earlier cases had begun in *Jamison* and *Largent. Murdock* had to rest, in part, on positions that could not be justified by the unreconstructed decisions of the earlier period. More than that, however, the result in *Murdock* depended upon overruling intervening judgments that accorded the earlier opinions the scope to which they were entitled and no more.

The new series of cases derived not from statutes which required licensing for the distribution of literature, but rather those which taxed the sale of such items. *Jones v. Opelika*[192] involved three such ordinances. In each instance a Jehovah's Witness was convicted for failure to pay the license tax for the sale of periodicals within the municipality. The unanimity that had pervaded the earlier judgments disappeared at this point. Mr. Justice Reed wrote for only five members of the Court in affirming the convictions. Although the attack was grounded on the free press and free speech provisions, it was the freedom of religion problem that dominated the opinions, of which there were four. Thus Mr. Justice Reed's opinion for the Court opened with an elegant statement of the older concept of the distinction between thought and action:

There are ethical principles of greater value to mankind than the guarantees of the Constitution, personal liberties which are beyond the power of government to impair. These principles and liberties belong to the mental and spiritual realm, where the judgments and decrees of mundane courts are ineffective to direct the course of man. The rights of which our Constitution speaks have a more earthy quality. They are not absolutes to be exercised independently of other cherished privileges, protected by the same organic instrument. Conflicts in the exercise of rights arise, and the conflicting forces seek adjustments in the courts, as do these parties, claiming on the one side the freedom of religion, speech and the press, guaranteed by the Fourteenth Amendment, and on the other the right to employ the sovereign power explicitly reserved to the State by the Tenth Amendment to ensure orderly living, without which the constitutional guarantees of civil liberties would be a mockery. Courts, no more than Constitutions, can intrude into the consciences of men or compel them to believe contrary to their faith or think contrary to their convictions; but courts are competent to adjudge the acts men do under color of a constitutional right, such as that of freedom of speech or of the press or the free exercise of religion, and to determine whether the claimed right is limited by other recognized powers, equally precious to mankind. So the mind and spirit of man remain forever free, while his actions rest subject to necessary accommodation to the competing needs of his fellows.[193]

Then the notion of balancing the interests was more specifically stated:

Believing, as this Nation has from the first, that the freedoms of worship and expression are closely akin to the illimitable privileges of thought itself, any legislation affecting those freedoms is scrutinized to see that the interferences allowed are only those appropriate to the maintenance of a civilized society. The determination of what limitations may be permitted under such an abstract test rests with the legislative bodies, the courts, the executive, and the people themselves, guided by the experience of the past, the needs of revenue for law enforcement, the requirements and capacities of police protection, the dangers of disorder, and other pertinent factors.[194]

Finally, he turned to the test of non-discrimination:

There is to be noted, too, a distinction between nondiscriminatory regulation of operations which are incidental to the exercise of religion or the freedom of speech or the press and those which are imposed upon the religious rite itself or the unmixed dissemination of information. . . .

When proponents of religious or social theories use the ordinary commercial methods of sales of articles to raise propaganda funds, it is a natural and proper exercise of the power of the State to charge reasonable fees for the privilege of canvassing. Careful as we may and should be to protect the freedoms safeguarded by the Bill of Rights, it is difficult to see in such enactments a shadow of prohibition of the exercise of religion or of abridgement of the freedom of speech or the press.[195]

He then abandoned the discrimination test:

> It may well be that the wisdom of American communities will persuade them to permit the poor and weak to draw support from the petty sales of religious books without contributing anything for the privilege of using the streets and conveniences of the municipality. Such an exemption, however, would be a voluntary, not a constitutionally enforced, contribution.[196]

But he returned to it:

> Nothing more is asked from one group than from another which uses similar methods of propagation. We see nothing in the collection of a non-discriminatory license fee, uncontested in amount, from those selling books or papers, which abridges freedoms of worship, speech or press. . . . The First Amendment does not require a subsidy in the form of fiscal exemption.[197]

Indeed, it might more properly be said that the first amendment prohibits such a subsidy where it is granted because of the religious nature of the activity conducted.

Mr. Chief Justice Stone's opinion did not segregate the speech and press issue from the religious issue. For him the license tax was invalid as involving the same kind of restraints that had been struck down when the sole issues involved licenses without taxes. No quarrel can be had with his conclusion about religious literature, so long as the same doctrine is applicable to non-religious literature. If the tax impinges on freedom of speech and press it does not do so any the less because the content of the information relates to religion; but it doesn't impinge any the more because the content is of a religious nature. He objected to the argument of nondiscrimination, on the ground that commercial solicitations do not receive the protection of the first amendment freedoms. But if he did not, in his own opinion, specifically say that the tax would be invalid even if the only protection were that of the freedom of religion clause, he joined Mr. Justice Murphy's opinion in which that position was taken.

Justices Black, Douglas, and Murphy, joined the Stone opinion. All four also joined the Murphy opinion in which, after agreeing that the tax was invalid because of its conflict with the guaranteed freedoms of press and speech, he went on to argue that the religion clause alone would sustain the position:

> Under the foregoing discussion of freedom of speech and freedom of the press, any person would be exempt from taxation upon the act of distributing information or opinion of any kind, whether political, scientific, or religious in character, when done solely in an effort to spread knowledge and ideas, with no thought of commercial gain. But there is another, and perhaps more precious, reason why these ordinances cannot constitutionally apply to petitioners. Important as free speech and a free press are to

a free government and a free citizenry, there is a right even more dear to many individuals—the right to worship their Maker according to their needs and the dictates of their souls and to carry their message or their gospel to every living creature. These ordinances infringe that right . . . .[198]

He had a little difficulty in stating his position as a doctrine, for qualifications to this ultimate freedom were acknowledged to exist: "There is here no contention that their manner of worship gives rise to conduct which calls for regulation, and these ordinances are not aimed at any such practices."[199] Inherent in this statement was the peculiar notion that the government may have a right to direct its limitation to what it considered to be an evil arising out of the religious nature of the practices involved. Such difficulties frequently inhere in those doctrines which would treat the separation and freedom clauses as distinct and unrelated guides to decision. Left unanswered by the Murphy approach is Mr. Justice Reed's proposition that "the First Amendment does not require a subsidy in the form of fiscal exemption." One can only judge from Murphy's opinion that he probably thought that it did.

The last, and somewhat curious, item about the case that calls for comment was the fourth opinion, signed jointly by Justices Black, Douglas and Murphy, in which they announced that they thought "this an appropriate occasion to state that we now believe that [*Gobitis*] . . . was wrongly decided."[200] The consequence of this announced change of position has already been considered.[201]

If the reversal of *Gobitis* by *Barnette* could not be attributed solely to a change in the personnel of the Court, the overruling of *Jones v. Opelika* by *Murdock v. Pennsylvania* has no other explanation. Rutledge replaced Byrnes on the Court between the 1941 and 1942 Terms and *Murdock* replaced *Jones*. Rehearing was granted in the *Jones* cases, after certiorari was granted in *Murdock*. And *Martin v. City of Struthers* which had been "dismissed on the ground that the record does not show that the federal question presented was properly preserved on appeal to the Court of Appeals . . ."[202] was reconsidered and probable jurisdiction noted.[203] This was the same Term at which the Court replaced *Gobitis* with *Barnette*.

The *Murdock* judgment was interwoven with those in two other cases decided at the same time: *Martin v. City of Struthers*[204] and *Douglas v. City of Jeannette*.[205] The majority opinion in *Murdock* was written by Mr. Justice Douglas; Mr. Justice Reed and Mr. Justice Frankfurter each wrote dissenting opinions. The Court was divided five to four.

The Douglas opinion first defined the actions of the Witnesses in the distribution of their literature as a religious rite:

> The hand distribution of religious tracts is an age-old form of missionary evangelism—as old as the history of printing presses. It has been a

potent force in various religious movements down through the years. This form of evangelism is utilized today on a large scale by various religious sects whose colporteurs carry the Gospel to thousands upon thousands of homes and seek through personal visitations to win adherents to their faith. It is more than preaching; it is more than distribution of religious literature. It is a combination of both. Its purpose is as evangelical as the revival meeting. This form of religious activity occupies the same high estate under the First Amendment as do worship in the churches and preaching from the pulpits. It has the same claim to protection as the more orthodox and conventional exercises of religion. It also has the same claim as the others to the guarantees of freedom of speech and freedom of the press.

The integrity of this conduct or behavior as a religious practice has not been challenged. Nor do we have presented any question as to the sincerity of petitioners in their religious beliefs and practices, however misguided they may be thought to be. Moreover, we do not intimate or suggest in respecting their sincerity that any conduct can be made a religious rite and by the zeal of the practitioners swept into the First Amendment.[206]

The difficulty with this approach is manifest. So long as the Court may say what is and what is not a proper religious practice—and it admitted that bigamy cannot be defended on that ground—it must reserve to itself exactly that discretion which it forbade to the city officials in *Cantwell*: it "authorize[s] an official to determine whether the cause is a religious one . . . thus establishing a censorship of religion."[207] It is somewhat difficult to understand where the Court gets this power of censorship which it said the Constitution denied non-judicial officials. The opinion also created another difficulty, especially for Mr. Justice Douglas. For if, as he later said in the released-time cases,[208] the state is forbidden to provide physical facilities for the execution of religious activities by reason of the separation clause, how is it that the state must make available its facilities to the "colporteurs"? In *Murdock* he said that the state not only may but must make such facilities available, and free of any license fee.

In the course of his opinion, Mr. Justice Douglas either wilfully or inadvertently limited, in order to reject, the argument of nondiscrimination:

The fact that the ordinance is "nondiscriminatory" is immaterial. The protection afforded by the First Amendment is not so restricted. A license tax certainly does not acquire constitutional validity because it classifies the privileges protected by the First Amendment along with the wares and merchandise of hucksters and peddlers and treats them alike. Such equality in treatment does not save the ordinance. Freedom of press, freedom of speech, freedom of religion are in a preferred position.[209]

But whence comes the justification for discrimination between speakers on religious subjects and peddlers of religious books, on the one hand, and speakers on non-religious subjects and peddlers of non-religious books, on the other? Does the first amendment command that special privileges be afforded those in the first category? And, if so, what of the separation clause? Clearly if the activities indulged by the colporteurs are protected by the freedom of press and speech provisions, they cannot be excluded from that protection because the subject of their activity is religion. Equally clear, if others engaged in the same activity but dealing with subjects other than religion are not protected by the free press and speech clauses, there is no warrant for the special right being granted to the colporteur.

Mr. Justice Douglas' final contribution was the destruction of a straw man:

> Plainly a community may not surpress, or the state tax, the dissemination of views because they are unpopular, annoying or distasteful. If that device were ever sanctioned, there would have been forged a ready instrument for the suppression of the faith which any minority cherishes but which does not happen to be in favor. That would be a complete repudiation of the philosophy of the Bill of Rights.[210]

The ultimate judgment in favor of the defendants is rested not alone on the provision for freedom of religion, but on that together with freedom of speech and press. It may well be that the judgment reached the correct result, but not because of the religious freedom clause.

The nondiscrimination argument that the majority opinion brushed off so lightly was stated differently in Mr. Justice Frankfurter's dissent than in Mr. Justice Reed's. For it was there recognized that tax exemption was not only a relief from an obligation, but if it was a relief from an obligation that all others must bear it amounted to the conferring of a benefit because of the religious quality of the exempted activity:

> It is strenuously urged that the Constitution denies a city the right to control the expression of men's minds and the right of men to win others to their views. But the Court is not divided on this proposition. No one disputes it. All members of the Court are equally familiar with the history that led to the adoption of the Bill of Rights and are equally zealous to enforce the constitutional protection of the free play of the human spirit. Escape from the real issue before us cannot be found in such generalities. The real issue here is not whether a city may charge for the dissemination of ideas but whether the states have power to require those who need additional facilities to help bear the cost of furnishing such facilities. Street hawkers make demands upon municipalities that involve the expenditure of dollars and cents, whether they hawk printed matter or other things. As the facts in these cases show, the cost of maintaining the peace, the additional demands upon governmental facilities for assuring security, involve outlays which have to be met. To say that the Constitution forbids the states to obtain the necessary revenue from the whole of a class that enjoys these benefits and facilities, when in fact no discrimination is suggested as

between the purveyors of printed matter and purveyors of other things, and the exaction is not claimed to be actually burdensome, is to say that the Constitution requires not that the dissemination of ideas in the interest of religion shall be free but that it shall be subsidized by the state. Such a claim offends the most important of all aspects of religious freedom in this country, namely, that of the separation of church and state.[211]

One need not agree with Mr. Justice Frankfurter that the license fee in *Murdock* was valid; but it is hard to reject the proposition that its invalidity could not turn on the religious nature of the defendants' activities.

This last distinction was emphasized by the second of this series of cases, *Martin v. City of Struthers*. It was emphasized most clearly by the difference between Mr. Justice Black's opinion for the Court and Mr. Justice Murphy's concurring opinion. The ordinance in question in *Struthers* made it "unlawful for any person distributing handbills, circulars or other advertisements to ring the door bell, sound the door knocker, or otherwise summon the inmate or inmates of any residence to the door for the purpose of receiving such handbills, circulars or other advertisements they or any person with them may be distributing."[212]

The appellant, a Jehovah's Witness, went from door to door in Struthers distributing handbills advertising a religious meeting. She was convicted of violation of the ordinance. She attacked the validity of the ordinance both as a violation of her rights of freedom of press and freedom of religion. Mr. Justice Black, writing for the majority, stated the question to be "whether the City, consistently with the federal Constitution's guarantee of free speech and press, possesses this power."[213] The Court held that freedom of speech and press was infringed, because the blanket nature of the ordinance prevented "dissemination of ideas." More refined protections of the householder might be valid. "The dangers of distribution can so easily be controlled by traditional legal methods, leaving to each householder the full right to decide whether he will receive strangers as visitors, that stringent prohibition can serve no purpose but that forbidden by the Constitution, the naked restriction of the dissemination of ideas."[214]

For the reason that the ordinance infringed the rights of freedom of speech and of the press, and for this reason alone, the conviction was upset.[215] If the doctrinal distinctions between this case and the *Murdock* case are hard for the reader to grasp, they were equally difficult for several members of the majority. Mr. Justice Murphy, joined by Justices Douglas and Rutledge, turned to the freedom of religion provision in succor of the defendant in *Struthers*. The reasoning may be summed up in two sentences. "There can be no question but that appellant was engaged in a religious activity when she was going from house to house in the City of Struthers distributing circulars advertising a meeting of those of her belief."[216] "Freedom of religion has a

higher dignity under the Constitution than municipal or personal convenience."[217]

Mr. Justice Frankfurter's opinion, labelled a dissent by the reporter but
not by the author, turned again to the problem of discrimination.

> The Court's opinion leaves one in doubt whether prohibition of all bell-
> ringing and door-knocking would be deemed an infringement of the con-
> stitutional protection of speech. It would be fantastic to suggest that a city
> has power, in the circumstances of modern urban life, to forbid house-to-
> house canvassing generally, but that the Constitution prohibits the inclu-
> sion in such prohibition of door-to-door vending of phylacteries or rosaries
> or of any printed matter. If the scope of the Court's opinion, apart from
> some of its general observations, is that this ordinance is an invidious dis-
> crimination against distributors of what is politely called literature, and
> therefore is deemed an unjustifiable prohibition of freedom of utter-
> ance, the decision leaves untouched what are in my view controlling con-
> stitutional principles, if I am correct in my understanding of what is held,
> and I would not be disposed to disagree with such a construction of the
> ordinance.[218]

This discrimination argument is the one that was answered by the Douglas'
opinion. It goes to discrimination between the exercise of speech and press
and other activities that fall outside that protected area. A stronger and dif-
erent argument in terms of "discrimination" is to be found in the opinion by
Mr. Justice Jackson in *Douglas v. City of Jeannette.*

In that case the majority had agreed to dismiss a suit to enjoin the enforce-
ment against Jehovah's Witnesses of the kinds of statutes that had been the
concern of the Court in this series of cases. In an opinion by Mr. Chief Justice
Stone, the Witnesses' complaint was dismissed and the relief sought denied
for want of equity jurisdiction. But it was to this opinion that Mr. Justice
Jackson's opinion, concurring in *Jeannette* and dissenting in *Murdock* and
Struthers, was appended. It should be noted that here the author of the
Court's opinion in the second flag-salute case also emphasized the difference
between protecting freedoms that belonged to all and giving special treatment
to those who asserted a religious ground for special treatment:

> In my view, the First Amendment assures the broadest tolerable exer-
> cise of free speech, free press, and free assembly, not merely for religious
> purposes, but for political, economic, scientific, news, or informational
> ends as well. When limits are reached which such communications must
> observe, can one go farther under the cloak of religious evangelism? Does
> what is obscene, or commercial, or abusive, or inciting become less so if
> employed to promote a religious ideology? I had not supposed that the
> rights of secular and non-religious communications were more narrow or
> in any way inferior to those of avowed religious groups.
>   It may be asked why then does the First Amendment separately men-

tion free exercise of religion? The history of religious persecution gives the answer. Religion needed specific protection because it was subject to attack from a separate quarter. . . . It was to assure religious teaching as much freedom as secular discussion, rather than to assure a greater license, that led to its separate statement.[219]

Mr. Justice Jackson might have noted, too, that the authors of the Constitution spelled out a qualification with reference to religious freedom in terms of separation that was not also applied to the other freedoms protected by the first amendment. Subsidy of the press, for example, is not specifically barred by the terms of the Constitution.

5. *Child Labor, Taxes, and Public Property. Prince v. Massachusetts*[220] put the new majority doctrine to the test and it failed. The defendant was convicted in Massachusetts for violation of that State's child labor laws. The violation consisted of supplying her nine-year old niece and ward with copies of Jehovah's Witness literature and taking her out into the streets in the evening to distribute it. Both the child and the defendant claimed to be ordained ministers in accordance with the creed of the Witnesses. The defendant attacked the application of the statute solely on the ground of the freedom of religion clause of the first amendment as incorporated in the fourteenth. Here then the religion clause was not, for purposes of decision, intertwined with those relating to speech and press.

The majority was caught between its stated principles of freedom of religion and its equally appealing duty to protect the right of the states to limit child labor. It chose the latter as the dominant consideration with the sole reason for its position that it believed the latter more important than the former. Mr. Justice Murphy would have none of this apostasy: "If the right of a child to practice its religion in that manner is to be forbidden by constitutional means, there must be convincing proof that such a practice constitutes a grave and immediate danger to the state or to the health, morals or welfare of the child."[221] But Mr. Justice Murphy was alone among the members of the Court. Three other justices did not join the majority opinion. They preferred the statement of position by Mr. Justice Jackson:

> This case brings to the surface the real basis of disagreement among members of this Court in previous Jehovah's Witness cases. . . . Our basic difference seems to be as to the method of establishing limitations which of necessity bound religious freedom.
>
> My own view may be shortly put: I think the limits begin to operate whenever activities begin to affect or collide with liberties of others or of the public. Religious activities which concern only members of the faith are and ought to be free—as nearly absolutely free as anything can be. But beyond these, many religious denominations or sects engage in collateral and secular activities intended to obtain means from unbelievers to sustain the worshippers and their leaders. They raise money, not merely by passing

the plate to those who voluntarily attend services or by contributions by their own people, but by solicitations and drives addressed to the public by holding public dinners and entertainments, by various kinds of sales and Bingo games and lotteries. All such money-raising activities on a public scale are, I think, Caesar's affairs and may be regulated by the state so long as it does not discriminate against one because he is doing them for a religious purpose, . . . in violation of other provisons of the Constitution.

The Court in the *Murdock* case rejected this principle of separating immune religious activities from secular ones in declaring the disabilities which the Constitution imposed on local authorities. Instead, the Court now draws a line based on age that cuts across both true exercise of religion and auxiliary secular activities.[222]

It is readily seen that Mr. Justice Jackson, who, from time to time, had appropriately stated the neutral principle that might be applied comes close to falling into the very error for which he had condemned others. By what standard could he distinguish between "true exercise of religion and auxiliary secular activities?" It is a line no more valid or reasonable than the ones he condemned. Thus, he departed from, or added to, the view he expressed in *Douglas v. City of Jeannette*, which would have brought him to the same conclusion he reached in *Prince*, but on sounder grounds. But at the same time he did state the nondiscrimination principle that properly should ground the decision of the Court.

Indeed, the distinction between "true exercise" and "auxiliary secular activities" in *Prince* was utilized to reach results with which Jackson disagreed in *Follett v. Town of McCormick*.[223] There a municipal ordinance imposed a tax on book agents and applied it to a Jehovah's Witness. The state courts sought to distinguish the earlier cases on the ground that here the defendant was local and, therefore, outside the category of itinerant preachers protected by the earlier cases.

The opinion written for the Court by Mr. Justice Douglas was simple in its construction. The Court need not, he said, draw the line between religious activities and non-religious activities with regard to the distributors of literature embracing the faith of the Jehovah's Witnesses: it had previously been decided that their activities fell on the religion side of the line. That made the question a narrow one for resolution: can the state tax the exercise of religion. The answer to that question, clearly, was that it cannot. Therefore, the tax in question was invalid. Q.E.D. Finally, in response to the dissent of Justices Roberts, Frankfurter, and Jackson:

> This does not mean that religious undertakings must be subsidized. The exemption from a license tax of a preacher who preaches or a parishioner who listens does not mean that either is free from all financial burdens of government, including taxes on, income or property. . . . But to say that they, like other citizens, may be subject to general taxation does not mean

that they can be required to pay a tax for the exercise of that which the First Amendment has made a high constitutional privilege.[224]

Why the tax involved in *Follett* was not a general tax imposed on all citizens who engaged in the activity indulged by Follett was never made clear. Mr. Justice Murphy's opinion was less ingenuous. He, too, felt it necessary to answer the contention of the dissent that the granting of exemption on the ground of religion was unconstitutional: "It is claimed that the effect of our decision is to subsidize religion. But this is merely a harsh way of saying that to prohibit the taxation of religious activities is to give substance to the constitutional right of religious freedom."[225]

The separate opinion of Roberts, Frankfurter, and Jackson returned to the hard problem: would not the exemption of activity from taxation on the ground of religion result in a subsidy to religion? If it would, would it not violate the separation clause? But strangely enough it was only the first question that was put. The separation clause remained a forgotten provision of the first amendment, even to the extent of its omission in the quotation of that amendment in the opinion.[226] But if the second question was not put explicitly, the problem it implicitly created was none the less there, even as the problem was stated by these dissenters:

> Follett is not made to pay a tax for the exercise of that which the First Amendment has relieved from taxation. He is made to pay for that for which all others similarly situated must pay—an excise for the occupation of street vending. Follett asks exemption because street vending is, for him, also part of his religion. As a result, Follett will enjoy a subsidy for his religion. He will save the contribution for the cost of government which everyone else will have to pay.
>
> . . .
>
> Unless the phrase "free exercise," embodied in the First Amendment, means that government must render service free to those who earn their living in a religious calling, no reason is apparent why the appellant, like every other earner in the community, should not contribute his share of the community's common burden of expense. In effect the decision grants not free exercise of religion, in the sense that such exercise shall not be hindered or limited, but, on the other hand, requires that the exercise of religion be subsidized. . . .
>
> . . .
>
> We cannot ignore what this decision involves. If the First Amendment grants immunity from taxation to the exercise of religion, it must equally grant a similar exemption to those who speak and to the press.
>
> . . .
>
> Not only must the court, if it is to be consistent, accord to dissemination of all opinion, religious or other, the same immunity, but, even in the field of religion alone, the implications of the present decision are startling. Multiple activities by which citizens earn their bread may, with equal propriety,

be denominated an exercise of religion as may preaching or selling religious tracts. Certainly this court cannot say that one activity is the exercise of religion and the other is not. The materials for judicial distinction do not exist. It would be difficult to deny the claims of those who devote their lives to the healing of the sick, to the nursing of the disabled, to the betterment of social and economic conditions, and to a myriad other worthy objects, that their respective callings, albeit they earn their living by pursuing them, are, for them, the exercise of religion. Such a belief, however earnestly and honestly held, does not entitle the believers to be free of contribution to the cost of government, which itself guarantees them the privilege of pursuing their callings without governmental prohibition or interference.[227]

The failure of this series of cases to arrive at a doctrine is due here, as elsewhere, to the failure to recognize the inseparable nature of the two religion clauses of the first amendment. Not even the different minorities of the Court, except by indirection, took notice of the unitary nature of the two clauses. That such recognition would lead to restriction on the proselyting efforts of the Jehovah's Witnesses was not a reason for rejecting the doctrine. If the obnoxious nature of a religious group's activities is not in itself a basis for inhibiting those activities, no more is it a basis for protecting them.

In each of the decisions relating to the right to license or tax, the Court dealt with the use of public streets. There were statements from time to time that an ordinance that permitted a private property owner to exclude the Witnesses or any other religious group from intruding would be sustained.[228] *Marsh v. Alabama*[229] presented the question of the distinction between private and public property for these purposes. An Alabama statute made it a crime to trespass on the property of another after warning not to do so.[230] The defendant was convicted of violating this law when she distributed literature in the usual manner of Jehovah's Witnesses within the confines of a "company town." The town of Chickasaw, Alabama, was owned by the Gulf Shipbuilding Corporation. The stores on the "business block" where the defendant engaged in her proselyting endeavors all contained notices to the effect that the property was private property and that no street vending or solicitation was permitted without authorization. The defendant was told that she would not be given authorization. When she persisted in her activities she was arrested.

The question, as put by Mr. Justice Black for the Court's majority, was "to decide whether a State, consistently with the First and Fourteenth Amendments, can impose criminal punishment on a person who undertakes to distribute religious literature on the premises of a company-owned town contrary to the wishes of the town's management."[231] The Court pointed out that if this were property belonging to a municipal corporation, there could be no doubt that the statute could not be validly applied to this defendant. Interestingly enough, Mr. Justice Black stated the barrier to such action in terms not restricted to religious literature: "[N]either a state nor a municipality can completely bar the distribution of literature containing religious or political ideas on its streets, sidewalks and public places or make the right to distribute dependent on a flat license tax or permit to be issued by an official who could deny it at will. . . . [A]n ordinance completely prohibiting the dissemination of ideas ón the city streets cannot be justified on the ground that the municipality holds legal title to them."[232] The Court held that the instant case could not be decided in terms of "the corporation's property interests."[233] The question did turn on the use to which the property was generally put. And, since "the town of Chickasaw does not function differently from any other town,"[234] the same rules would be applied to it as to municipal corporations of more public nature. Despite this statement of position, the Court modified the doctrine on which the conclusion was based. The test was a balancing of interests:

> When we balance the Constitutional rights of owners of property against those of the people to enjoy freedom of press and religion, as we must here, we remain mindful of the fact that the latter occupy a preferred position. . . . In our view the circumstance that the property rights to the premises where the deprivation of liberty, here involved, took place, were held by others than the public, is not sufficient to justify the State's permitting a corporation to govern a community of citizens so as to restrict their fundamental liberties and the enforcement of such restraint by the application of a state statute.[235]

Two items should be underlined. First, that the rights involved included freedom of the press as well as freedom of religion. Second, that the rights imposed on are spoken of as those belonging to the community to receive the information rather than that of the individual to disseminate it.

Mr. Justice Frankfurter agreed that so long as the law relating to distribution in municipal streets was what it was, the ownership of this property by the Gulf corporation should not afford a basis for distinction. It was Mr. Justice Reed who wrote the dissenting opinion. He was joined by Mr. Chief Justice Stone and Mr. Justice Burton. In the course of his opinion he chose the unfortunate but none the less frequent approach of a dissenter of making the majority opinion stand for a much broader proposition than it undertook to claim for itself: "What the present decision establishes as a principle is that one may remain on private property against the will of the owner and contrary to the law of the state so long as the only objection to his presence is that he is exercising an asserted right to spread there his religious views."[236] He admitted that the Court might in the future be more restrictive in the application of that "principle," but said that in doing so it would have to rely on the drawing of arbitrary lines rather than resting on the existing doctrine that distinguished public from private property.

In the companion case of *Tucker v. Texas*[237] the Court split along the same lines. As Mr. Justice Black said, in speaking for the majority:

The only difference between this case and *Marsh* v. *Alabama* is that here instead of a private corporation, the Federal Government owns and opererates the village. This difference does not affect the result. Certainly neither Congress nor Federal agencies acting pursuant to Congressional authorization may abridge the freedom of press and religion safeguarded by the First Amendment. True, under certain circumstances it might be proper for security reasons to isolate the inhabitants of a settlement, such as Hondo Village, which houses workers engaged in producing war materials. But no such necessity and no such intention on the part of Congress or the Public Housing Authority are shown here.[238]

Saia v. New York[239] contains a strange bit of irony in the development of guides in this area. The case involved the conviction of a Jehovah's Witness who utilized a sound truck for the dissemination of his doctrine without the license required by state law. He had previously received permission to use loud-speaking equipment in the city park on designated Sundays. After complaints about the noise, the police refused permission for further activity of this sort. The defendant proceeded to act without the license. He was arrested and convicted of violating the ordinance requiring a license. His appeal to the Supreme Court asserted that the ordinance "violated appellant's rights of freedom of speech, assembly, and worship under the Federal Constitution."[240] But Mr. Justice Douglas held the ordinance "unconstitutional on its face" only on the ground that "it establishes a previous restraint on the right of free speech in violation of the First Amendment which is protected by the Fourteenth Amendment against State action."[241] The irony lies in the fact that the religious freedom in this area which, as has been shown, derived from the rights accorded freedom of press and speech, is now suggested as the appropriate base on which the rights of free speech should rest: "Unless we are to retreat from the firm positions we have taken in the past, we must give freedom of speech in this case the same preferred treatment that we gave freedom of religion in the *Cantwell* case . . . ."[242] The *Cantwell* case, of course, decided only the want of power of a state to determine what was religious activity. There are qualifications here, too, on the freedom to use loudspeakers. The absolute right is less than absolute, even though "loud-speakers are today indispensable instruments of effective public speech."[243] "Noise can be regulated by regulating decibals. The hours and place of public discussion can be controlled."[244] It is thus once again the Court's function to balance interests and determine for itself which interest is to be given priority. But it must recognize the preferred position of the first amendment freedoms.

Mr. Justice Frankfurter, joined by Justices Reed and Burton, dissented on the ground that the community has the right to reserve its public parks for uses that do not interfere with other persons' utilization of the facilities. Admitting the possibility of an arbitrary and capricious application of the ordinance, they found none here and were unwilling to indulge the assumption that such action would occur. Mr. Justice Jackson's solo dissent is of interest with reference to the religion issue, with which neither the majority nor the other dissenters really dealt. It is of interest because it presented a dilemma that the Court did not consider then and has since left unresolved:

> But the Court points out that propagation of his religion is the avowed and only purpose of appellant and holds that Lockport cannot stop the use of loud-speaker systems on its public property for that purpose. If it is to be treated as a case merely of religious teaching, I still could not agree with the decision. Only a few weeks ago we held that the Constitution prohibits a state or municipality from using tax-supported property "to aid religious groups to spread their faith." *McCollum* v. *Board of Education*, 333 U.S. 203. Today we say it compels them to let it be used for that purpose. In the one case the public property was appropriated to school uses; today it is public property appropriated and equipped for recreational purposes. . . . And I cannot see how we can read the Constitution one day to forbid and the next day to compel use of public tax-supported property to help a religious sect spread its faith.[245]

He then pointed out the lack of discrimination and rejected the notion that the Court rather than the local authorities should balance the interests involved and reach a conclusion as to which was better for the community.

The dilemma, of course, derives from the failure of the Court to treat the religion clauses in the unitary fashion that would require religion to be ruled out as a measure of state action. But once again, it should be noted that *Saia*, like many of its predecessors, did not at the time of its promulgation rest on either of the religion clauses in the first amendment, despite the fact that they were offered as a basis for decision by the appellant.

The problem of sound trucks and free speech was not put to rest in *Saia*. In *Kovacs v. Cooper*,[246] decided at the next term, the problem reappeared in a context in which there was no religious element. The Court could not agree on an opinion resolving the question whether a Trenton ordinance that forbade the emission of "loud and raucous" noises by sound equipment was validly applied to the appellant. Mr. Justice Reed's opinion, in which the Chief Justice and Mr. Justice Burton joined, distinguished *Saia* on the ground that the Trenton statute did contain an appropriate standard, the absence of which made the *Saia* ordinance invalid. Mr. Justice Frankfurter's concurring opinion rested on the position he had taken in *Saia*. He used the opinion as a vehicle for reviewing the meaning of the proposition that first amendment rights were to be treated as "preferred rights." Mr. Justice Jackson's concurrence was also repetitive of his position in *Saia* and he joined Mr. Justice Black's dissenting view that *Saia* was effectively overruled by this decision. Black's position rested on the fact that the charge levelled at the defendant did not state the standard of the ordinance so that the defendant was condemned simply for using a loud-speaker on the public streets. He retained the views of the majority in *Saia*.

It is perhaps to be suggested that, although neither *Saia* nor *Kovacs* said so, the difference in result in *Kovacs* may well have rested on the fact that the latter case did not involve any element of religious proselyting.

After a short interval the Court's attention was shifted from the problem of noise to the problem of the use of public property for proselyting, the issue that Mr. Justice Jackson raised in *Saia*. The first of this new series was *Niemotko v. Maryland*.[247] But the decision there was simple. In that case, without any statutory warrant, the defendants were arrested for making proselyting speeches in a public park without having secured permission to do so. "[R]arely has any case been before this Court which shows so clearly an unwarranted discrimination in a refusal to issue . . . a license. . . . The conclusion is inescapable that the use of the park was denied because of the City Council's dislike for or disagreement with the Witnesses or their views."[248] Although all the justices did not concur in Mr. Chief Justice Vinson's opinion, they all concurred in the result: the conviction was invalid under the equal protection clause of the fourteenth amendment. It could as appropriately have been based on the religion clauses of the first amendment properly construed to prohibit classification in terms of religion.

The second case, *Kunz v. New York*,[249] proved a bit more difficult, although it could have been disposed of in the same manner by recognition of the suggested principle of the first amendment. For there, the City of New York had an ordinance that prohibited the holding of "public worship" meetings on the city streets without a permit. It was thus a classification in terms of religion and, therefore, invalid on its face, on proper analysis. The Court indeed rested on the first amendment in upsetting a conviction for preaching without a permit after a permit had been refused. But it concealed which provisions of the first amendment were relied on. The defendant was not a Jehovah's Witness, incidentally, but one whose "calling" also required him to "go out on the highways and byways and preach the word of God"[250] and to preach it in a manner that called for "scurrilous attacks on Catholics and Jews."[251] He had earlier received a permit to engage in his "calling," but the police refused renewal after experience indicated that his preaching against Jews and Catholics in New York City had stirred his listeners to threatened violence. Mr. Chief Justice Vinson, on behalf of the Court, struck down the ordinance as "clearly invalid as a prior restraint on the exercise of First Amendment rights" because it gave "an administrative official discretionary power to control in advance the right of citizens to speak on religious matters on the streets of New York."[252] Again, however, as in the comparison of the *Saia* and *Kovacs* cases, one might draw the inference that the religious element played a role from the fact that in *Feiner v. New York*,[253] a conviction was affirmed for engaging in somewhat similar activities where the speaker was inciting the crowd on issues not religious in nature. It is also true, however, that the *Feiner* case can be distinguished from the *Kunz* case in that *Kunz* involved problems of prior restraint and *Feiner* did not. Strangely enough, however,

Mr. Chief Justice Vinson, who wrote both opinions for the Court, made no mention of *Kunz* at all in his *Feiner* opinion, nor of the *Feiner* case in his *Kunz* opinion.

Mr. Justice Frankfurter's concurring opinion included all three cases: *Niemotko*, *Kunz*, and *Feiner*. After setting out the relevant precedents, and analyzing the various relevant factors, he concluded that the *Niemotko* conviction was invalid because of the discriminatory application of the ordinance and that the *Kunz* conviction was invalid because of the lack of standards in the ordinance granting administrative authority to license. Neither of these grounds is necessarily concerned with the religion clauses of the first amendment. But he did say of the *Kunz* case, in language as ambiguous as that of the majority: "Such a standard, considering the informal procedure under which it is applied, too readily permits censorship of religion by the licensing authorities. *Cantwell v. Connecticut* . . . ."[254]

Mr. Justice Jackson's dissent was biting. He would sustain the requirement of the permit in *Kunz*. He refused to treat the ordinance in a vacuum; there was cause here for the denial. The *Chaplinsky* case made clear to him that the kind of epithets that Kunz was accustomed to using were evils which the state had the right to abate. To assert that the state was required to draft an ordinance or a statute that would be valid against all claims of freedom of speech was to ask more of the state legislative bodies than the Court itself was competent to provide: "It seems hypercritical to strike down local laws on their faces for want of standards when we have no standards."[255] But Jackson, too, was talking of problems of speech and not of religion in his opinion. Little may be derived from *Niemotko* and *Kunz* about the proper application of the religion clauses of the first amendment. But these clauses were relevant to the next case to come before the Court.

The decision in *Fowler v. Rhode Island*[256] was not difficult to reach on the basis of any of the doctrines that have been suggested. The conviction of the Jehovah's Witness in that case was for violation of an ordinance that forbade speeches in public parks. Mr. Justice Douglas' opinion for the majority would seem to suggest that the statute was invalid in its application to religious meetings. But by reason of counsel's admission at oral argument, it was not necessary to assert any such doctrine:

> [I]t was conceded at the trial that this meeting was a religious one. On oral argument before the Court the Assistant Attorney General further conceded that the ordinance, as construed and applied, did not prohibit church services in the park. Catholics could hold mass in Slater Park and Protestants could conduct their church services there without violating the ordinance. Church services normally entail not only singing, prayer, and other devotionals but preaching as well. Even so, those services would not be barred by the ordinance. That broad concession, made in oral argument, is fatal to Rhode Island's case. For it plainly shows that a religious service of Jehovah's Witnesses is treated differently than a religious service of other

sects. That amounts to the state preferring some religious groups over this one. In *Niemotko* . . . we had a case on all fours with this one . . . .[257]

But the opinion went on to eschew the power to decide what was "a religious practice or activity" except in a "narrow" class of cases that the Court did not distinguish, such as *Davis v. Beason* and *Reynolds v. United States,* because, it is submitted, it has produced no doctrine capable of distinguishing them. Mr. Justice Frankfurter would have rested the result entirely on the equal protection clause and Mr. Justice Jackson concurred only in the result. It should be noted that the notion of the utility of the equal protection clause in this area is akin to the suggested thesis of this paper, except that in its application to this case it involved discrimination among religions rather than the problem of classification in terms of religion.

The public park problem was revived in *Poulos v. New Hampshire.*[258] Poulos had been denied a permit to conduct religious services in a public park in Portsmouth, New Hampshire. He held the services anyway and was prosecuted and convicted. The New Hampshire high court affirmed the conviction on the ground that if the license had been improperly denied, the proper remedy was by mandamus or other such writ directing the issuance of the license. This Poulos refused to seek. The opinion of the majority makes some things clear. The mere requirement of a license is not unconstitutional as violative either of the free speech or religion clauses:

> The principles of the First Amendment are not to be treated as a promise that everyone, with opinions or beliefs to express may gather around him at any public place and at any time a group for discussion or instruction. It is a *non sequitur* to say that First Amendment rights may not be regulated because they hold a preferred position in the hierarchy of the constitutional guarantees of the incidents of freedom. This Court has never so held and indeed has definitely indicated the contrary. It has indicated approval of reasonable nondiscriminatory regulation by governmental authority that preserves peace, order and tranquility without deprivation of the First Amendment guarantees of free speech, press and the exercise of religion. When considering specifically the regulation of the use of public parks, this Court has taken the same position. . . . In [*Kunz* and *Saia*] the ordinances were held invalid, not because they regulated the use of the parks for meeting and instruction but because they left complete discretion to refuse the use in the hands of officials.[259]

It went on to hold that Poulos was not denied any constitutional rights by the requirement that he seek correction of erroneous action by the licensing authorities in the Courts. Mr. Justice Frankfurter's opinion would rest solely on this ground. Justices Black and Douglas, who dissented, rested their positions wholly on the free speech provisions of the first amendment and rejected both arguments of the majority as an authorization of censorship of speech.

7

THE TRIAL OF "SAINT GERMAIN"

What may be the insoluble problem under any theory of the meaning of the first amendment religion clauses was brought to the Court in *United States v. Ballard*.[260] There, the leaders of the "I Am" movement were prosecuted for using the mails to defraud. The indictment alleged that Mrs. Ballard, "alias Saint Germain, Jesus, Joan of Arc, Lotus Ray King, Chanera,"[261] and others, had secured moneys by misrepresentations and had used the mails in doing so. Among the misrepresentations alleged

> were claims that Guy W. Ballard had attained a supernatural state of immortality; that all the Ballards had been selected as divine messengers through whom the teachings of St. Germain and other "ascended masters" would be communicated to mankind; that the Ballards had the power to conquer disease, death, old age, poverty, and misery; that they could cure and had cured persons of physical ailments; that they had the power to precipitate from the air money and other material riches; that they had received divine visitations from St. Germain and other supernatural entities who dictated the books published by defendants; that St. Germain had appeared in person before Charles Sindelar who had painted the saint's portrait; that books, charts, and phonograph records issued by defendants had special salutary qualities which would be transmitted to purchasers; that since a catclysm was about to engulf the earth it was wiser to give money to defendants than to invest it in banks, homes, insurance, etc. . . . .[262]

The Government demonstrated that a large number of people to whom these representations were made contributed sums of moneys to the defendants, in the form of donations and as the purchase price for the various books, records, and paintings that were represented to have supernatural qualities.

In a political society dedicated to the proposition that, so far as the state is concerned, there are no religious truths, how could the Government prove the falsehood of the representations? As the respondents pointed out, the representations of the Ballards were not different in kind from those made by longer-established religions who receive money from their membership. Thus, the promise of attainment of old age and immortality is compared with the representations in the Old Testament that Adam reached the age of 930, Moses, 120, Methuselah, 969, and the statement in Matthew: "Verily I say unto you. There be some standing here, which shall not taste of death, till they see the Son of man coming in his kingdom."[263] With regard to the divine appointment and selection of the Ballards, the comparison is again made with the Bible and with the Mormons:

> It is not without precedent for one to claim revelation. The Bible from start to finish conclusively proves and establishes that very thing. See: Amos 3:7; Jeremiah 1:5; Genesis 5:22; Genesis 6. . . .
> Christ Himself was a revelator. (John 12:49–50.) . . .
> Direct revelation is not the basis of all Christian faiths. Some churches, for example the Roman Catholic, claim direct lineal authority from Christ. Some, for example, the Lutheran, claim authority on the direction given by Jesus to preach the gospel as expressed in Mark 16:15–18. But direct revelation is the basis of authority for other religions, for example, Church of Jesus Christ of the Latter Day Saints, also known as Mormons.[264]

Similar comparisons were made with regard to the teachings allegedly conducive to attainment of eventual salvation. Reference is made to the Athanasian Creed[265] and to Mark: "He that believeth and is baptized shall be saved; but he that believeth not shall be damned."[266] The sale of literature was analogized to the distribution of "the 'Christian Science Monitor,' 'Christian Science Sentinel,' Catholic 'Tidings,' Catholic 'Messenger,' the Mormon 'Improvement Era,' and other church publications. Hymn books and manuals are used in practically every religion."[267] Again, with reference to healing, the respondents drew comparisons with other religions not under attack for misrepresentations: "Why were they not as justified in believing and stating this to be the fact as those who conduct the Shrine at Lourdes, France, and St. Anne's de Beaupre, at Quebec, Canada?"[268] "As defined by Mary Baker Eddy the religion she founded is 'divine methaphysics'; it is 'the scientific system of divine healing'; it is 'the law of God, the law of good, interpreting and demonstrating the divine principle and rule of universal harmony.' "[269] "Again we realize that in the Bible we are taught that healings through others than Christ have occurred. (Mark 16:18)."[270] The analogy with reference to "precipitation" was weaker. The best that the defense could come up with was two quotations from the New Testament: "what I do all men shall do and greater things than these shall ye do. John 14:12 . . .";[271] " 'And I say unto you, ask and it shall be given you; seek and ye shall find; knock and it shall be opened unto you.' (Luke 11:9)"[272]

Again with reference to the prediction of a cataclysm, the defendants asserted a parallel with more widely accepted religions. Among those referred to were the Books of Malachi and Matthew:

> In the Book of Malachi, 4:1-5, it is stated that the "earth shall burn as an oven and all the proud and the wicked shall burn as stubble, but unto you that fear My Name shall the Son of Righteousness arise with healing in his wings and ye shall go forth and grow up as calves of the stall."
> In the New Testament, Jesus, in speaking of his second coming, stated: "There shall not be left here one stone upon another that shall not be thrown down." (Matthew 24.) See, also, Isaiah 2 and 24.[273]

The problem presented by the case is patent. Religious belief could not excuse criminal activity. But a person could not be prosecuted for his religious belief. The truth of the representations cannot be measured by the courts any more than the truth of the representations of the more established religions could be determined by law. And yet the very essence of the charge required proof of the falsehood of the assertions.

The trial court, in consultation with counsel for both sides attempted to find a way out. The method suggested was to measure only the good faith of the defendants in making these representations. The trial court addressed the jury:

> Now, gentlemen, here is the issue in this case:
> First, the defendant in this case made certain representations of belief in a divinity and in a supernatural power. Some of the teachings of the defendants, representations, might seem extremely improbable to a great many people. For instance, the appearance of Jesus to dictate some of the works that we have had introduced in evidence, as testified to here at the opening transcription, or shaking hands with Jesus, to some people that might seem highly improbable. I point that out as one of the many statements.
> Whether that is true or not is not the concern of this Court and is not the concern of the jury—and they are going to be told so in their instructions. As far as this Court sees the issue, it is immaterial what these defendants preached or wrote or taught in their classes. They are not going to be permitted to speculate on the actuality of the happening of those incidents. Now, I think I have made that as clear as I can. Therefore, the religious beliefs of these defendants cannot be an issue in this court.
> The issue is: Did these defendants honestly and in good faith believe those things? If they did, they should be acquitted. I cannot make it any clearer than that.
> If these defendants did not believe those things, they did not believe that Jesus came down and dictated, or that St. Germain came down and dictated, did not believe the things that they wrote, the things that they

preached, but used the mail for the purpose of getting money, the jury should find them guilty. Therefore, gentlemen, religion cannot come into this case.[274]

Despite the acquiescence of defense counsel in this statement, the Court of Appeals for the Ninth Circuit reversed the jury verdict. It "held that the question of the truth of the representations concerning respondents' religious doctrines or beliefs should have been submitted to the jury."[275] All nine justices of the Supreme Court were convinced that the Court of Appeals was in error in this position. They were not agreed as to the proper method of treating the problem.

Mr. Justice Douglas, speaking for the majority, held that the truth of respondents' allegations with reference to their religion could not be submitted to any trier of fact:

> Many take their gospel from the New Testament. But it would hardly be supposed that they could be tried before a jury charged with the duty of determining whether those teachings contained false representations. The miracles of the New Testament, the Divinity of Christ, life after death, the power of prayer are deep in the religious convictions of many. If one could be sent to jail because a jury in a hostile environment found those teachings false, little indeed would be left of religious freedom. . . . Man's relation to his God was made no concern of the state. . . . The religious views espoused by respondents might seem incredible, if not preposterous, to most people. But if those doctrines are subject to trial before a jury charged with finding their truth or falsity, then the same can be done with the religious beliefs of any sect. When the triers of fact undertake that task, they enter a forbidden domain.[276]

The result was that the judgment upsetting the convictions was reversed and the case remanded to the appellate court for consideration of the other grounds asserted by the defendants as bases for reversal.[277]

Mr. Chief Justice Stone, joined by Justices Roberts and Frankfurter, would have sustained the conviction. He found the Court's discussion irrelevant to the issues presented by the case. The issue of the truth of the religious beliefs was withdrawn from the jury. No question was presented as to whether the facts occurred. The sole question submitted to the jury was "whether petitioners [sic] honestly believed that they had occurred, with the instruction that if the jury did not so find, then it should return a verdict of guilty. On this issue the jury, on ample evidence that respondents were without belief in the statements which they had made to their victims, found a verdict of guilty. The state of one's mind is a fact as capable of fraudulent misrepresentation as is one's physical condition or the state of his bodily health."[278]

Mr. Justice Jackson would have reversed the conviction. His opinion, unconvincing to his brethren, sets out principles that are hard to refute and are not adequately answered by either of the other opinions in the case:

In the first place, as a matter of either practice or philosophy I do not see how we can separate an issue as to what is believed from considerations as to what is believable. The most convincing proof that one believes his statements is to show that they have been true in his experience. Likewise, that one knowingly falsified is best proved by showing that what he said happened never did happen. How can the Government prove these persons knew something to be false which it cannot prove to be false? If we try religious sincerity severed from religious verity, we isolate the dispute from the very considerations which in common experience provide its most reliable answer.

In the second place, any inquiry into intellectual honesty in religion raises profound psychological problems. . . . If religious liberty includes, as it must, the right to communicate such experiences to others, it seems to me an impossible task for juries to separate fancied ones from real ones, dreams from happenings, and hallucinations from true clairvoyance. . . . Religious symbolism is even used by some with the same mental reservations one has in teaching of Santa Claus or Uncle Sam or Easter bunnies or dispassionate judges. It is hard in matters so mystical to say how literally one is bound to believe the doctrine he teaches and even more difficult to say how far it is reliance upon a teacher's literal belief which induces followers to give him money.

. . .

Prosecutions of this character easily could degenerate into religious persecution. I do not doubt that religious leaders may be convicted of fraud for making false representations on matters other than faith or experience, as for example if one represents that funds are being used to construct a church when in fact they are being used for personal purposes. But that is not this case, which reaches into wholly dangerous ground. When does less than full belief in a professed credo become actionable fraud if one is soliciting gifts or legacies? Such inquiries may discomfort orthodox as well as unconventional religious teachers, for even the most regular of them are sometimes accused of taking their orthodoxy with a grain of salt.

I would dismiss the indictment and have done with this business of judicially examining other people's faiths.[279]

It would seem to be Jackson's position that the dilemma presented by *Ballard* was unresolvable. Under such circumstances, a criminal conviction should hardly be permitted to stand. A slightly more difficult case might be presented in a civil suit for damages, but the answer should probably be the same.

8

THE SCHOOL BUS CASE:

THE PRECEDENT OF BYRON'S JULIA

In the cases that preceded *Everson v. Board of Education*,[280] the Court had · seldom undertaken to supply content to that part of the first amendment concerned with separation. The Court had, theretofore, more or less assumed that the freedom provision was separable from the separation clause and, therefore, could be treated in the same manner as those referring to speech, press, and assembly. Thus, when *Everson* came before them, the justices were able to write on a comparatively clean slate, at least insofar as their judgments rather than their dicta were concerned. They fully utilized the opportunity: the *Everson* problem was canvassed by three separate opinions covering seventy-four pages. The Court was divided five to four.

The litigation arose out of payments made by the township of Ewing, New Jersey to parents of parochial school children in reimbursement for the costs of transportation of those children to their school. A taxpayer of the township took exception to the payments and brought suit to effectuate his objections. The payments had been made for this transportation pursuant to a state statute and a resolution of the school board of Ewing purportedly issued in accordance with the statute. The exact language of each is relevant to an evaluation of the various opinions. The statute read as follows:

> Whenever in any district there are children living remote from any school-house, the board of education of the district may make rules and contracts for the transportation of such children to and from school, including the transportation of children to and from school other than a public school, except such school as is operated for profit in whole or in part.
>
> When any school district provides any transportation for public school children to and from school, transportation from any point in such established school route to any other point in such established school route shall be supplied to school children residing in such school district in

going to and from school other than a public school, except such school
as is operated for profit in whole or in part.

Nothing in this section shall be so construed as to prohibit a board of
education from making contracts for the transportation of children to a
school in an adjoining district when such children are transferred to the
district by order of the county superintendent of schools, or when any
children shall attend school in a district other than that in which they shall
reside by virtue of an agreement made by the respective boards of education.[281]

It should be noted that the statute, in authorizing payment for school transportation, drew a line only between students attending non-profit institutions
and those attending schools operated for profit in whole or in part. The resolution in contest was differently phrased: "The Transportation Committee
recommended the Transportation of Pupils of Ewing to the Trenton High and
Pennington High and Trenton Catholic Schools, by way of public carriers
as in recent years. On motion of Mr. R. Ryan, seconded by Mr. French, the
same was adopted."[282] The language of the resolution is only once referred
to in the Court's opinion in *Everson*. Unlike the statute, it draws the line in
terms of two public high schools and Trenton Catholic schools, on the one
hand, and all other schools on the other. It was the difference in construction
of this resolution that really caused the difference in result between the opinions of Mr. Justice Black for the majority and Mr. Justice Jackson for himself and Mr. Justice Frankfurter. Mr. Justice Rutledge's dissenting opinion,
joined by Mr. Justice Burton as well as Justices Frankfurter and Jackson,
would reach a different conclusion from the majority without regard to the
terms of the school board's resolution.

Mr. Justice Black's opinion first disposes of the argument that the payments
were illegal because they required the taking of some persons' property for
the private use of others. This, it will be recalled, was the major emphasis of
the appellants in the *Cochran* case and the argument was quickly disposed of on
that authority. "It is much too late to argue that legislation intended to facili-
tate the opportunity of children to get a secular education serves no public
purpose. . . . The same thing is no less true of legislation to reimburse needy
parents, or all parents, for payment of the fares of their children so that they
can ride in public busses to and from schools rather than run the risk of
traffic and other hazards incident to walking or 'hitchhiking.' "[283]

With reference to the first amendment problem, Black started with a review
of the history and precedents of the amendment's religion clauses. The conclusion to be derived from these sources was set out:

The "establishment of religion" clause of the First Amendment means
at least this: Neither a state nor the Federal Government can set up a

church. Neither can pass laws which aid one religion, aid all religions, or prefer one religion over another. Neither can force nor influence a person to go to or to remain away from church against his will or force him to profess a belief or disbelief in any religion. No person can be punished for entertaining or professing religious beliefs or disbeliefs, for church attendance or non-attendance. No tax in any amount, large or small, can be levied to support any religious activities or institutions, whatever they may be called, or whatever form they may adopt to teach or practice religion. Neither a state nor the Federal Government can, openly or secretly, participate in the affairs of any religious organizations or groups and *vice versa*. In the words of Jefferson, the clause against establishment of religion by law was intended to erect "a wall of separation between church and State." *Reynolds* v. *United States* . . . . [284]

In applying this principle to the case before the Court, Mr. Justice Black came close to the test that is advocated here: that the legislation in question cannot classify in terms of religion. The language that he used contains italicizied matter, matter that the Court itself intended to emphasize, that goes directly to this proposition:

New Jersey cannot consistently with the "establishment of religion" clause of the First Amendment contribute tax-raised funds to the support of an institution which teaches the tenets and faith of any church. On the other hand, the language of the amendment commands that New Jersey cannot hamper its citizens in the free exercise of their own religion. Consequently, it cannot exclude individual Catholics, Lutherans, Mohammedans, Baptists, Jews, Methodists, Non-believers, Presbyterians, or the members of any other faith, *because of their faith, or lack of it*, from receiving the benefits of public welfare legislation. While we do not mean to intimate that a state could not provide transportation only to children attending public schools, we must be careful, in protecting the citizens of New Jersey against state-established churches, to be sure that we do not inadvertently prohibit New Jersey from extending its general state law benefits to all its citizens without regard to their religious belief.[285]

In short, a classification in terms of public and non-public schools would be valid. A classification in terms of religion would be invalid. This is again emphasized in the Court's opinion at a later point. In sustaining the validity of the New Jersey action in question, the opinion said: "Its legislation, as applied, does no more than provide a general program to help parents get their children, regardless of their religion, safely and expeditiously to and from accredited schools."[286]

In order to reach this conclusion, the majority had to ignore the fact that the resolution as adopted distinguished in terms of religion in the very manner that the Court said a State could not do. The explanation for this was contained in a footnote that suggested that, for purposes of the litigation, the

Court was reading the resolution to authorize payment of bus fares for all children travelling the requisite distance and not merely those attending public and Catholic schools: "Although the township resolution authorized reimbursement only for parents of public and Catholic school pupils, appellant does not allege, nor is there anything in the record which would offer the slightest support to an allegation, that there were any children in the township who attended or would have attended, but for want of transportation, any but public and Catholic schools."[287]

It was apparently because he read the record differently that Mr. Justice Jackson dissented in a separate opinion. He began his opinion with what has become a famous quotation:

> [T]he undertones of the opinion, advocating complete and uncompromising separation of Church from State, seem utterly discordant with its conclusions yielding support to their commingling in educational matters. The case which irresistibly comes to mind as the most fitting precedent is that of Julia who, according to Byron's reports, "whispering 'I will ne'er consent,'—consented."[288]

But it was really the record and not doctrine that separated these two opinions. Mr. Justice Jackson complained about the New Jersey statute on the ground that it improperly drew a line between schools that were operated for profit and those that were not, in determining what students should be reimbursed for their transportation costs. Whether that is a proper line need not be discussed here; certainly, however, that is not a line drawn explicitly in terms of religion. The more appropriate objection was to the application of the statute pursuant to the resolution: "children are classified according to the schools they attend and are to be aided if they attend the public schools or private Catholic schools, and they are not allowed to be aided if they attend private secular schools or private religious schools of other faiths."[289] The question, therefore, according to Jackson was: "Is it constitutional to tax this complainant to pay the costs of carrying pupils to Church schools of one specified denomination?"[290] Given that question, there could, of course, be but one answer. But it must be emphasized that the question that the majority answered was really a different one: whether it was constitutional to include parochial school students in the payment of transportation when the state purportedly was paying the transportation of all students? It was the difference in the questions that so clearly called for different answers. But this was not altogether clear from the language of the Jackson opinion which suggested that any payment to parochial schools might fall under the ban, whether the contribution was going to all schools or not. For Jackson, aid to a "Church school is indistinguishable . . . from rendering the same aid to the Church itself."[291] He reached this conclusion on the basis of his characterization of the Catholic schools as "the most vital part of the Roman Catholic Church."[292] And, he went on, "It is of no importance in this situation whether the beneficiary of this expenditure of tax-raised funds is primarily the parochial school and incidentally the pupil, or whether the aid is directly bestowed on the pupil with indirect benefits to the school."[293] Despite this language, however, when it came to stating the guiding rule, he, too, resorted to the question of discrimination or classification in religious terms as the ultimate test:

> It seems to me that the basic fallacy in the Court's reasoning, which accounts for its failure to apply the principles it avows, is in ignoring the essentially religious test by which beneficiaries of this expenditure are selected. A policeman protects a Catholic, of course—but not because he is a Catholic; it is because he is a man and a member of our society. The fireman protects the Church school—but not because it is a Church school; it is because it is property, part of the assets of our society. Neither the fireman nor the policeman has to ask before he renders aid "Is this man or building identified with the Catholic Church?" But before these school authorities draw a check to reimburse for a student's fare they must ask just that question, and if the school is a Catholic one they may render aid because it is such, while if it is of any other faith or is run for profit, the help must be withheld.[294]

It should be apparent that this is the test that Mr. Justice Black also stated and the test that is proposed by this paper to be applicable not only to questions of separation but to questions of freedom as well, because the two are not separable.

Mr. Justice Rutledge would take a more restrictive view: "The prohibition broadly forbids state support, financial or other, of religion in any guise, form or degree. It outlaws all use of public funds for religious purposes."[295] He would appear to ban payment for bus transportation to parochial school children even if authorized to be made to all school children. "Legislatures are free to make, and courts to sustain, appropriations only when it can be found that in fact they do not aid, promote, encourage or sustain religious teaching or observances, be the amount large or small. No such finding has or could be made in this case."[296] He denied that under the facts hypothesized "failure to provide it [bus transportation] would make the state unneutral in religious matters, discriminating against or hampering such children concerning public benefits all others receive."[297] "Of course discrimination in the legal sense does not exist. The child attending the religious school has the same right as any other to attend the public school."[298] He rejected the analogy to police and fire protection as irrelevant. He then admitted that he could place his dissent on narrower grounds. He would find the exclusion in the statute of children attending schools run for profit an invalid classification, as well as the limitation in the resolution to Catholic and public school students: "There is no showing that there are no other private or religious schools in this populous district. I do not think it can be assumed that there were none."[299] But he preferred the broader ground, one that, in fact, makes the application of the two religion clauses a matter for the discretion of the Court.

9

RELEASED TIME:

THE PRECEDENT OF JULIA AGAIN

In 1954, the Supreme Court noted that "education is perhaps the most important function of state and local governments. . . . To separate them‑ [school children] from others of similar age and qualifications solely because of their race generates a feeling of inferiority as to their status in the community that may affect their hearts and minds in a way unlikely ever to be undone."[300] Thus was segregation by race within the nation's public schools made illegal. The fact that it had existed from the institution of public school systems in those states that still retained it in 1954 was thought not to be a barrier to its destruction. The Court had earlier dealt with similar problems concerning not race but religion. The history of segregating school children within their schools, for part of the time, by religious classifications was not so ancient as the South's color segregation, but it was far more widespread in the United States. It was this system of segregation that was first challenged in the Supreme Court in *McCollum v. Board of Educ.*[301] If the furor that resulted from the *Brown* case did not cause the Court to limit its holding— indeed it has expanded its application—the furor that followed the *McCollum* case had a different effect: most of what *McCollum* had done was undone a few years later in *Zorach v. Clauson.*[302] If it is not fair to say that the Supreme Court follows the election returns, it may nonetheless be true that there are times when some of its members may seem to anticipate them.

In Champaign, Illinois, students were released from their public school classes for a period of thirty or forty-five minutes each week so that they might take religious instruction. This instruction was given on the school premises by teachers approved but not employed by the public school. It was given in the regular classrooms to those students whose parents indicated that they desired their children to take such instruction. Students who did not take religious instruction were required to leave their classrooms to continue their secular studies elsewhere in the building. Student attendance at the religious classes was reported to the school authorities.

Mrs. McCollum, who chose not to have her child take such religious training, sued to enjoin the continuance of the system on the ground that it violated the first and fourteenth amendments by utilization of the compulsory education law to compel attendance at religious courses. Mr. Justice Black, writing for the Court, had little difficulty in disposing of the case. "Pupils compelled by law to go to school for secular education are released in part from their legal duty upon the condition that they attend the religious classes. This is beyond all question a utilization of the tax-established and tax-supported public school system to aid religious groups to spread their faith. And it falls squarely under the ban of the First Amendment (made applicable to the States by the Fourteenth) as we interpreted it in *Everson*. . . ."[303]

He emphasized two grounds as the basis for the conclusion reached by the Court: "Here not only are the State's tax-supported public school buildings used for the dissemination of religious doctrines. The State also affords sectarian groups an invaluable aid in that it helps to provide pupils for their religious classes through the use of the State's compulsory public school machinery. This is not separation of Church and State."[304]

Mr. Justice Frankfurter found the problem somewhat more complex in the opinion he wrote for himself and Justices Jackson, Rutledge, and Burton, the last two of whom also joined the majority opinion. He reviewed the history of the secularization of education and of the development of various "released-time" programs. He emphasized the uniqueness of each of the released-time programs and suggested that each would have to be dealt with on its merits. But he also emphasized the destructiveness of the Champaign released-time program, in language that suggests the psychological terms used later in the *School Segregation* cases:

> The fact that this power has not been used to discriminate is beside the point. Separation is a requirement to abstain from fusing functions of Government and of religious sects, not merely to treat them all equally. That a child is offered an alternative may reduce the constraint; it does not eliminate the operation of influence by the school in matters sacred to the conscience and outside the school's domain. The law of imitation operates, and non-conformity is not an outstanding characteristic of children. The result is an obvious pressure upon children to attend. . . . The children belonging to these non-participating sects will thus have inculated in them a feeling of separatism when the school should be the training ground for habits of community, or they will have religious instruction in a faith which is not that of their parents. As a result, the public school system of Champaign actively furthers inculcation in the religious tenets of some faiths, and in the process sharpens the consciousness of religious differences at least among some of the children committed to its care. These are consequences not amenable to statistics. But they are precisely the consequences against which the Constitution was directed when it prohibited the Government common to all from becoming embroiled, however innocently,

in the destructive religious conflicts of which the history of even this country reports some dark pages.[305]

Mr. Justice Jackson, who concurred in the Frankfurter opinion, also wrote an opinion of his own. He questioned the standing of the parent to maintain the action, since there could be no showing of monetary cost to the community in maintaining the system. But his greater complaint was the possibility that the injunction would now be in the sweeping terms requested by the plaintiff:

> While we may and should end such formal and explicit instruction as the Champaign plan and can at all times prohibit teaching of creed and catechism and ceremonial and can forbid forthright proselyting in the schools, I think it remains to be demonstrated whether it is possible, even if desirable, to comply with such demands as plaintiff's completely to isolate and cast out of secular education all that some people may reasonably regard as religious instruction. . . . While I agree that the religious classes in volved here go beyond permissible limits, I also think the complaint demands more than plaintiff is entitled to have granted. So far as I can see this Court does not tell the State court where it may stop, nor does it set up any standards by which the State court may determine that question for itself.
>
> The task of separating the secular from the religious in education is one of magnitude, intricacy and delicacy. To lay down a sweeping constitutional doctrine as demanded by complainant and apparently approved by the Court, applicable alike to all school boards of the nation, "to immediately adopt and enforce rules and regulations prohibiting all instruction in and teaching of religious education in all public schools," is to decree a uniform, rigid and, if we are consistent, an unchanging standard for countless school boards representing and serving highly localized groups which not only differ from each other but which themselves from time to time change attitudes. It seems to me that to do so is to allow zeal for our own ideas of what is good in public instruction to induce us to accept the role of a super board of education for every school district in the nation.[306]

As it turned out, Mr. Justice Jackson's fears proved groundless. No one accepted the decree suggested by Mrs. McCollum as binding on non-participants: the local schools reacted to the judgment with the same disrespect for the "law of the land" as the Southern schools reacted to the *School Segregation* cases. The phrase "super board of education" was readily picked up to castigate the Court for its work. And the Court lacked that consistency that Jackson feared it might display.

Mr. Justice Reed's lonesome dissent raised questions as to the ground for the majority action. He could not tell whether the evil was the use of the school buildings, the release of students during school hours, the assistance of teachers in keeping attendance and securing permission cards, or the action of higher authority in arranging the program. What seemed to be rhetorical questions to some turned out to be ones of very real importance when the problem was later re-examined. He would rely here, as he chose not to do in the *School Segregation* cases, on the "well-recognized and long-established practices" as proof of validity of the Illinois program: "This is an instance where, for me, the history of past practices is determinative of the meaning of a constitutional clause, not a decorous introduction to the study of its text. The judgment should be affirmed."[307]

Once again, as in the flag-salute cases, a lone dissent was to turn into a majority. Between *McCollum* and *Zorach*, Justices Murphy and Rutledge were replaced by Justices Clark and Minton. But again the new justices were not themselves enough to make the difference. Mr. Chief Justice Vinson and Justices Douglas and Burton, who had been in the majority in *McCollum* were also in the majority in *Zorach*; indeed, Mr. Justice Douglas wrote the latter opinion. Between the two cases there also came the condemnation of almost all the organized church groups in the country and no little criticism from the legal periodicals.[308]

The invitation of Justices Frankfurter and Jackson to treat the various released-time programs individually rather than in gross was accepted by the New York courts. They found the New York City released-time program valid in spite of the *McCollum* case. Factually, the only difference between the Champaign and New York City programs was that the students released to take religious education in New York left the school premises in order to do so. Mr. Justice Douglas' opinion almost conceded this to be the only distinction, but regarded it as a distinction that made a difference:

> In the *McCollum* case the classrooms were used for religious instruction and the force of the public school was used to promote that instruction. Here, as we have said, the public schools do no more than accommodate their schedules to a program of outside religious instruction. We follow the *McCollum* case. But we cannot expand it to cover the present released-time program unless separation of Church and State means that public institutions can make no adjustments of their schedules to accommodate the religious needs of the people. We cannot read into the Bill of Rights such a philosophy of hostility to religion.[309]

The author of the *McCollum* opinion was unable to recognize the difference. Mr. Justice Black's dissent pointed out: "As we attempted to make categorically clear, the *McCollum* decision would have been the same if the religious classes had not been held in the school buildings."[310] "*McCollum* . . . held that Illinois could not constitutionally manipulate the compelled classroom hours of its compulsory school machinery so as to channel children into sectarian classes."[311] The compulsion exerted in *Zorach* was neither less nor different from that held invalid in *McCollum*. He concluded: "State help to religion injects political and party prejudices into a holy field. It too often substitutes force for prayer, hate for love, and persecution for persuasion. Government should not be allowed, under cover of the soft euphemism of 'co-operation,' to steal into the sacred area of religious choice."[312]

Mr. Justice Frankfurter, who joined Jackson's dissenting opinion, also provided one of his own. The difference between closing the school completely and allowing some to be relieved of the obligation to attend on condition that they attend religious instruction was too clear to permit the former to be used as authority for the latter. He charged that the reliance on the absence in the record of any proof of coercion was footless, for the case came up on pleadings and the complaint asserted coercion.

Mr. Justice Jackson's opinion put the issue quickly, and assuming the continued vitality of McCollum, or even without it, unanswerably: "Stripped to its essentials, the plan has two stages: first, that the State compel each student to yield a large part of his time for public secular education; and, second, that some of it be 'released' to him on condition that he devote it to sectarian religious purposes."[313] He also, more than adequately, disposed of the lack of coercion argument:

> The greater effectiveness of this system over voluntary attendance after school hours is due to the truant officer who, if the youngster fails to go to the Church school, dogs him back to the public schoolroom. Here schooling is more or less suspended during the "released time" so the non-religious attendants will not forge ahead of the churchgoing absentees. But it serves as a temporary jail for a pupil who will not go to Church. It takes more subtlety of mind than I possess to deny that this is governmental constraint in support of religion. It is as unconstitutional, in my view, when exerted by indirection as when exercised forthrightly.[314]

Of the distinction of the McCollum case, he said:

> The distinction attempted between that case and this is trivial, almost to the point of cynicism, magnifying its nonessential details and disparaging compulsion which was the underlying reason for invalidity. A reading of the Court's opinion in that case along with its opinion in this case will show such difference of overtones and undertones to make it clear that the McCollum case has passed like a storm in a teacup. The wall which the Court was professing to erect between Church and State has become even more warped and twisted than I expected. Today's judgment will be more interesting to students of psychology and of the judicial processes than to students of constitutional law.[315]

Not much need be added to that proposition except to suggest that even students of constitutional law would prefer the honest and open retraction utilized in the other cases to the patently disingenuous method of revision used in Zorach.

10

OF CZAR AND COMMISSAR

On June 6, 1960, after a decade and a half of litigation, the question of the right to the use and possession of the premises at Nos. 13–15 East 79th Street in New York City was unanimously decided by the Supreme Court of the United States.[316] Such questions of proprietary interests in real property are not the usual grist for the Supreme Court mill. Indeed, Mr. Justice Jackson had told his brethren some eight years earlier, when the issue was first before the Court, that the question of the use of these premises was none of its business.[317] His brethren thought otherwise then and announced adherence to the same position in 1960, because the premises in question constitute the St. Nicholas Cathedral of the Russian Orthodox Greek Catholic Church.

Basically, the contest that came twice to the Supreme Court involved the conflicting claims of Leonty Turkevitch and Benjamin Fedchenkoff, and their respective successors, to the right of occupancy of the Cathedral. The former asserted his rights by reason of his election to the office of Metropolitan of All America and Canada and Archbishop of New York by a convention of American bishops, clergymen, and laymen, acting as a "sobor" or governing body of the Church. The latter's claims derived from an appointment as Archbishop of the Archdiocese of North America and the Aleutian Islands by the Patriarch *locum tenens* of Moscow and All Russia and his Holy Synod.

The resolution of the conflict demanded an understanding of church history easier to assert than to prove.[318] The best that can be made from the record[319] and briefs follows. From 987 A.D. until about the time of the fall of Constantinople to the Turks in 1453, the Russian Church was part of the Church of Constantinople, ruled by the Ecumenical Patriarch there. When the center of Eastern orthodoxy was taken by unbelievers, the Russian Church asserted its independent right to choose its own metropolitan, without securing the approval of the Ecumenical Patriarch, and did so. In 1598, when the Russian and Constantinople branches of the church were reconciled, the agreement was predicated on a recognition of the independent authority of the first Patriarch of Moscow and All Russia. After the fall of Moscow to later-day unbelievers, the American branch of the Russian church, which had originated in Alaska and the Aleutians in 1793, sought to make history repeat itself by establishing its independence, but failed to satisfy the Supreme Court of the validity of such historical judgment.

After the control and domination of the Church by the Czar was broken by the 1917 revolution, the administration of the Church was recognized during the short-lived, if long-lamented, Kerensky regime. In 1917–18, at a sobor, the patriarchate, which had been abolished by Peter the Great, was restored. The Patriarch replaced the procurator of the Czar as the head of the Holy Synod. The sobor was established, or re-established, as the fount of authority. But this reform, like others of the time, was soon jeopardized by the continuing events of the revolution, and Tikhon, former Archbishop of North America who had been elected Patriarch at the 1917–18 sobor, and the Holy Synod issued a ukase in anticipation of the difficulties that they foresaw. Among other things, this ukase of November 20, 1920, provided that:

> [I]f the highest Church Administration itself with the Holy Patriarch at the head would for any reason discontinue their church-administrative activity, the Diocesan Bishop will immediately get into communication with the Bishops of his neighboring Dioceses for the purpose of organizing a superior instance of Church Authority for several dioceses which would find themselves in similar conditions. (Be it in the form of a temporary highest Church Government or a Metropolitan District or even otherwise.)[320]

In 1922, as anticipated, the Patriarch was arrested. Various attempts to set up a "living church" more consonant with the tenets of the Communist dogmas failed. But until 1927, the patriarchate as established by the 1917–18 sobor, was not functioning.

Purportedly in pursuance of the ukase of Tikhon, quoted above, a sobor was held in Detroit in 1924, pursuant to which the American Dioceses set up an American church, independent of the Russian hierarchy, until such time as that hierarchy should be freed from the control of the Russian state.[321] In 1945, a ukase was issued by the Moscow church authorities calling for the reunion of the American and Russian churches. This was rejected by the American congregations at their Cleveland Sobor of 1946. American delegates to a 1945 sobor in Moscow failed to arrive in time to participate in the actions that resulted in the 1945 ukase. In the meantime, the contest between the American church appointee and the Russian church appointee over the control of the Cathedral in New York and other churches was carried to the courts and litigated and relitigated.[322]

At this point, and at the instigation of the American church, the New York legislature intervened:

> Article 5-C was added to the Religious Corporations Law of New York in 1945 and provided both for the incorporation and administration of Russian Orthodox churches. Clarifying amendments were added in 1948. The purpose of the article was to bring all the New York church, formerly subject to the administrative jurisdiction of the Most Sacred Governing Synod in Moscow or the Patriarch of Moscow, into an administratively autonomous metropolitan district. That district was North American in area, created pursuant to resolutions adopted at a sobor held at Detroit in 1924. This declared autonomy was made effective by a further legislative requirement that all the churches formerly administratively subject to the Moscow synod and partriarchate should for the future be governed by the ecclesiastical body and hierarchy of the American metropolitan district.[323]

The New York courts gave effect to this statute and judgment was entered in favor of the American church designate to control the use of the Cathedral.[324]

The Supreme Court, speaking through Mr. Justice Reed, held the statute unconstitutional. It rejected the New York Court of Appeals' thesis, which it described:

> Since certain events of which the Court took judicial notice indicated to it that the Russian Government exercised control over the central church authorities and that the American church acted to protect its pulpits and faith from such influences, the Court of Appeals felt that the Legislature's reasonable belief in such conditions justified the State in enacting a law to free the American group from infiltration of such atheistic or subversive influences.[325]

Mr. Justice Reed recognized the power to punish even ecclesiastics for subversion, but there was no subversive action by any ecclesiastic involved here. He followed, after extensive quotation, the decision of *Watson v. Jones*,[326] although that case involved no constitutional issue and applied a "general federal common law" which has since been recognized to have no validity. The contest over church property resulting from the Presbyterian church schism involved in *Watson* was decided on the ground that, in a hierarchical church, questions as to the beneficial use of church property must be determined according to the decision of "the highest of these church judicatories."[327] The Court's conclusion was, therefore, readily reached:

> Ours is a government which by the "law of its being" allows no statute, state or national, that prohibits the free exercise of religion. There are occasions when civil courts must draw lines between the responsibilities of church and state for the disposition or use of property. Even in those cases when the property right follows as an incident from decisions of the

church custom or law on ecclesiastical issues, the church rule controls.
This under our Constitution necessarily follows in order that there may
be free exercise of religion.[328]

This conclusion rested, however, on an earlier proposition of more doubtful
validity: "We find nothing that indicates a relinquishment of this power by
the Russian Orthodox Church."[329] And, again, "Nothing indicates that either
the Sacred Synod or the succeeding Patriarchs relinquished that authority or
recognized the autonomy of the American church."[330] Both of these statements failed to recognize the possibility that the authority of the American
church to make itself independent was properly grounded on the authorization of the Patriarch Tikhon quoted above.[331] Although the opinion noted
the existence of this authorization it did little more than that.

The opinion pointed out that the factual issue that would have to be resolved in order to decide that question was not answered by the New York
Court of Appeals: "The court did consider 'whether there exists in Moscow
at the present time a true central organization of the Russian Orthodox
Church capable of functioning as the head of a free international religious
body.' It concluded that this aspect of the controversy had not been sufficiently
developed to justify a judgment upon that ground."[332] The New York courts
need not have resolved the question in light of their decision in favor of the
American church. But if the Tikhon ukase was to be given any effect, the Supreme Court would have to know the answer to that question before it could
decide in favor of the Russian hierarchy.

Mr. Justice Frankfurter, writing for himself and Justices Black and Douglas, the last of whom joined the majority opinion as well, reached the same
conclusion. He, too, found in *Watson v. Jones* the guiding principle, but he
went further in limiting the power of the legislature to act:

> [W]hen courts are called upon to adjudicate disputes which, though gen-
> erated by conflicts of faith, may fairly be isolated as controversies over
> property and therefore within judicial competence, the authority of courts
> is in strict subordination to the ecclesiastical law of a particular church prior
> to a schism. *Watson* v. *Jones* .... This very limited right of resort to courts
> for determination of claims, civil in their nature, between rival parties
> among the communicants of a religious faith is merely one aspect of the
> duty of courts to enforce the right of members in an association, temporal
> or religious, according to the laws of that association. ...
>
> Legislatures have no such obligation to adjudicate and no such
> power .... [333]

Unlike the majority, however, he went on to deal with the argument that the
Russian patriarch was not the leader of the Church. But he did not deal
specifically with the effect of the Tikhon ukase:

Finally, we are told that the present Moscow Patriarchate is not the true superior church of the American communicants. . . . Even were there doubt about this it is hard to see by what warrant the New York Legislature is free to substitute its own judgment as to the validity of Patriarch Alexi's claim and to disregard acknowledgement of the present Patriarch by his coequals in the Eastern Confession, the Patriarchs of Constantinople, Alexandria, Antioch, and Jerusalem, and by religious leaders throughout the world, including the present Archbishop of York.[334]

He also disposed of Mr. Justice Jackson's argument in dissent that there was here in question only the right to possession of realty and, therefore, the controversy was within the control of the State of New York:

St. Nicholas Cathedral is not just a piece of real estate. It is no more that than is St. Patrick's Cathedral or the Cathedral of St. John the Divine. A cathedral is the seat and center of ecclesiastical authority. St. Nicholas Cathedral is an archepiscopal see of one of the great religious organizations. What is at stake here is the power to exercise religious authority. That is the essence of this controversy. It is that even though the religious authority becomes manifest and is exerted through authority over the Cathedral as the outward symbol of a religious faith.[335]

For Mr. Justice Jackson, in dissent, the religious freedom issue was nonexistent. The controversy was solely one over real property—an action of ejectment to be determined by state law. "The fact that property is dedicated to a religious use cannot, in my opinion, justify the Court in sublimating an issue over property rights into one of deprivation of religious liberty . . . ."[336] He also interjected the suggestion that the limitations that the first amendment religion clauses impose on the national government may be greater than those applicable to the states through the fourteenth amendment. It is an idea that has not received Court sanction but has found adherents among students of the subject.[337]

On remand, the New York courts again reached their original conclusion, but rested this time on judicial power rather than the validity of the New York statute.[338] On certiorari, the Supreme Court reversed in a per curiam decision on the ground that in *Kedroff* the Court had ruled that the right of use and possession "was 'strictly a matter of ecclesiastical government,' and as such could not constitutionally be impaired by a state statute . . . ."[339] It followed, for the 1960 Court, that what could not be done by statute could not be done by judicial decree. There were no dissents noted.

There is nothing in any of the opinions to suggest why church property is entitled to more favorable or less favorable treatment than other property. There is a suggestion in Mr. Justice Frankfurter's opinion that the issue should be treated in the same way that a question arising over the property of any "voluntary association" would be.[340] This, too, was the direction of

the Jackson dissent. Especially difficult to comprehend is the compulsory with-
drawal of state power in favor of "ecclesiastical government" when the very
issue in the case was which of two ecclesiastical governments was entitled to
make the decision. If the Supreme Court has the power to choose between
the two, which it did, why is a state precluded from doing so? Finally, the possible anomaly of the decision is worth noting, although it would be difficult
indeed to resolve: the reading of the first amendment that precludes the
State of New York from applying its law because of the necessity of separation
of church and state may result in the domination of a church in this country
by the government of a foreign and unfriendly power.[341]

11

NEVER ON SUNDAY

Sunday closing legislation has had a long history and most of it was set out at length in one or another of the opinions rendered by the Court on the subject of its constitutionality during the 1960 Term. Indeed, in the four cases disposed of by opinion, the Court contributed well over two hundred pages to the discussion of the subject[342]—this despite the fact that the problem had been presented to the Court many times in recent years in cases disposed of by orders of dismissal for want of a substantial federal question.[343] Nor was there an absence of older Supreme Court opinions on the subject.[344] It should be obvious, therefore, that any exegesis here must take the form of synopsis rather than expansive analysis.

The first time the Court had a serious look at a closing regulation, it involved Thursdays rather than Sundays. In *Richardson v. Goddard*,[345] a carrier had delivered cargo at a wharf in Boston; the cargo was thereafter destroyed by fire. The consignee brought a suit in admiralty against the ship for improper delivery on the ground that "by the appointment of the Govenor of Massachusetts, [Thursday] was kept and regarded by the citizens as 'a day of fasting, humiliation, and prayer,' " during which the people of Massachusetts abstained "from all secular work."[346] The consignees urged that the delivery was, therefore, improper. Mr. Justice Grier noted, first, that the Massachusetts high court had ruled that the only day on which business was suspended was Sunday; second, that even with reference to the ban on secular business on Sunday by both Church and State, "*lading and unlading of ships in maritime commerce*"[347] was an exception; and, third, that while it was customary in Massachusetts to enforce "the most rigid observance of the Lord's day as a Sabbath," they did not enforce fast days or prayer days in order that the people of Massachusetts "might enjoy liberty of conscience."[348] Thus, drawing a distinction between the sabbath and mere fast days or prayer days, the Court ruled that the delivery was proper.

During the same term of court, Mr. Justice Grier delivered another opinion in admiralty, in which he rejected a defense that because the damaged ship was transporting goods on Sunday, the vessel was precluded from collecting for the injury resulting from collision with an obstruction to navigation negligently left in the water by the defendant.[349] The reasons for his conclusion were two: (1) "The law relating to the observance of Sunday defines a duty of the citizen to the State, and to the State only. For a breach of this duty he is liable to the fine or penalty imposed by the statute, and nothing more."[350] (2) "We have shown, in an opinion delivered at this term, that in other Christian countries, where the observance of Sundays and other holidays is enforced by both Church and State, the sailing of vessels engaged in commerce, and even their lading and unlading, were classed among the works of necessity, which are excepted from the operation of such laws."[351]

Hennington v. Georgia[352] sustained a state law that prohibited the operation of railroad trains within the state on Sundays, against the contention that the state statute was in conflict with the commerce clause. The first Mr. Justice Harlan found the law to be merely a proper exercise of the police power that did not burden interstate commerce improperly. "In our opinion there is nothing in the legislation in question which suggests that it was enacted with the purpose to regulate interstate commerce, or with any other purpose than to prescribe a rule of civil duty for all who, on the Sabbath day, are within the territorial jurisdiction of the State. It is none the less a civil regulation because the day on which the running of freight trains is prohibited is kept by many under a sense of religious duty"[353]—this despite Mr. Justice Brewer's statement a few years earlier that "the laws respecting the observance of the Sabbath" offered proof "that this is a Christian nation."[354] *Petit v. Minnesota*[355] sustained a state Sunday closing law against an attack on the ground that it violated the equal protection clause. In that case the statute exempted works of "necessity or charity" and specifically provided that barbering was not a work of "necessity." Petit, convicted for keeping open a barber shop on Sunday, was brushed off in an opinion by Mr. Chief Justice Fuller, in which he said, inaccurately but none the less conclusively: "We have uniformly recognized state laws relating to the observance of Sunday as enacted in the legitimate exercise of the police powers of the State. The subject was fully considered in *Hennington* . . . and it is unnecessary to go over the ground again."[356] He was correct, however, in observing that "innumerable decisions of the state courts have sustained the validity of such laws."[357] *Soon Hing v. Crowley*,[358] in which the Court disposed not of a Sunday closing law, but rather of a law limiting the hours during which the complaining laundryman might work in his laundry, also contained relevant dicta: "Laws setting aside Sunday as a day of rest are upheld, not from any right of the government to legislate for the promotion of religious observances, but from its right to protect all persons from the physical and moral debasement which comes from uninterrupted labor."[359] These declamations on behalf of the protection of the poor working people would have a more sincere ring today if "freedom of contract" had not been so invulnerable a concept at the time these decisions were reached. The dicta might also be more persuasive were the holdings of more certain vitality.

This, then, was the record of Supreme Court activity on which the Court could rely when the Sunday closing cases of the 1960 Term were brought before them.

In the first of the four cases, *McGowan v. Maryland,*[360] the attack was made on the Maryland statute by seven employees of a discount store who had been arrested and convicted for selling "a three-ring loose-leaf binder, a can of floor wax, a stapler and staples, and a toy submarine"[361] on Sunday in violation of the statute. Three arguments were made: 1) that the statute denied the defendants the equal protection of the laws; 2) that the statute was void for vagueness; and 3) that "the statutes are laws respecting an establishment of religion or prohibiting the free exercise thereof."[362] It is only the last that will be considered here, but it should be noted that the Court ruled against the defendants on all three.

The opinion for the Court was written by Mr. Chief Justice Warren and joined by Justices Black, Clark, Brennan, Whittaker, and Stewart. Over Mr. Justice Douglas' dissent, the Court held that the appellants lacked standing to raise any question of infringement of religious freedom. The opinion, therefore, purported to deal only with the "establishment" question. The difficulties were patent. Clearly the Sunday closing laws in their origins were promulgated to accomplish religious objectives; even today the closing laws are beneficial to those religions that require the observance of Sunday as part of their religious precepts.

First, the Chief Justice accorded a wider function to the establishment clause than would those who contend for its application only in furtherance of the freedom clause.[363] "If the purpose of the 'establishment' clause was only to insure protection for the 'free exercise' of religion, then what we have said above concerning appellants' standing to raise the 'free exercise' contention would appear to be true here. [*I.e.,* appellants would lack standing to attack the validity of the statute on the basis of the first amendment.] However . . . the establishment of a religion was equally feared because of its tendencies to political tyranny and subversion of civil authority."[364] The appellants have standing because they have suffered economic injury "allegedly due to the imposition on them of the tenets of the Christian religion."[365]

The Chief Justice then acknowledged that the original Sunday laws "were motivated by religious forces."[366] But even "before the eighteenth century, nonreligious arguments for Sunday closing began to be heard more distinctly and the statutes began to lose some of their totally religious flavor."[367] Today, the "proponents of Sunday closing legislation are no longer exclusively representatives of religious interests."[368] What then of the statute that combines objectives of a secular nature with those of religious character? The Court started here with the proposition "that the 'Establishment' Clause does not ban federal or state regulation of conduct whose reason or effect merely happens to coincide or harmonize with the tenets of some or all religions."[369] From there it went by imperceptible steps to the proposition that the secular reasons were dominant rather than coordinate:

> In light of the evolution of our Sunday Closing Laws through the centuries, and of their more or less recent emphasis upon secular considerations, it is not difficult to discern that as presently written and administered, most of them, at least, are of a secular rather than of a religious character, and that presently they bear no relationship to establishment of religion as those words are used in the Constitution of the United States.
> . . . The present purpose and effect of most of them is to provide a uniform day of rest for all citizens; the fact that this day is Sunday, a day of particular significance for the dominant Christian sects, does not bar the State from achieving its secular goals. To say that the States cannot prescribe Sunday as a day of rest for these purposes solely because centuries ago such laws had their genesis in religion would give a constitutional interpretation of hostility to the public welfare rather than one of mere separation of church and State.[370]

Turning to the Maryland statute in question, the Court put a unique twist on the various exemptions provided by Maryland law. Having disposed of the contention that these exemptions do not result in invalid classification for purposes of the equal protection clause or undue vagueness under the due process clause, the Court pointed out that they were not merely exemptions for "works of charity or necessity" which would comport with the early interpretations of the religious restrictions on Sunday labor, but rather reveal that they are "clearly to be fashioned for the purpose of providing a Sunday atmosphere of recreation, cheerfulness, repose and enjoyment. Coupled with the general proscription against other types of work, we believe that the air of the day is one of relaxation rather than one of religion."[371] Here, at last, exceptions proved the rule.

There remained, then, only the need to demonstrate why, if the objective of the law was assurance of relaxation from work, the statute could specify the day rather than provide that persons must take off at least one day in seven. The answer was two-fold. First, it was desirable that a single day should be chosen so that it might be shared by the family and community. Second, the designation of the day would make the enforcement of the law more feasible than the suggested alternative.[372]

The concluding paragraph of the opinion then asserted a principle not diverse from that proposed in this thesis, that if the basis for action were religious in nature the statute would be invalid:

> Finally, we should make clear that this case deals only with the constitutionality of § 521 of the Maryland statute before us. We do not hold that Sunday legislation may not be a violation of the "Establishment" Clause if it can be demonstrated that its purpose—evidenced either on the face of the legislation, in conjunction with its legislative history, or in its operative effect—is to use the State's coercive power to aid religion.[373]

In *Gallagher v. Crown Kosher Super Market*,[374] Warren's opinion commanded only a plurality and not a majority of the Court. Justices Brennan and Stewart, who helped form the majority in *McGowan* were in dissent in *Gallagher*. The Court disposed of the equal protection and establishment arguments largely on the basis of *McGowan*. The fact that the Massachusetts law spoke in terms of observation of "the Lord's Day" proved to have no impact on the judgment: "It would seem that the objectionable language is merely a relic."[375] Equally impotent was the fact that here—unlike *McGowan* where the lower courts had found that the purpose of the statute was secular —"the three-judge district court found that Massachusetts had no legitimate secular interest in maintaining Sunday closing."[376] So far as the "freedom of religion" issues raised in *Gallagher* were concerned, they were disposed of on the basis of the opinion for the same four Justices in *Braunfeld v. Brown*,[377] where the "allegations" were "similar" but even more "grave."[378]

In *Braunfeld*, in the opinion which commanded the votes of four members of the Court, the Chief Justice disposed of the equal protection and establishment arguments on the grounds advanced in *McGowan* and *Two Guys from Harrison-Allentown Inc. v. McGinley*,[379] where the freedom issue was not relevant. Thus, the emphasis in *Braunfeld* was on the question whether a Sunday closing law was invalid as applied to Orthodox Jewish storekeepers who were compelled, by their religion, to remain closed on Saturday. In sustaining the validity of the legislation, the Chief Justice began by asserting the proposition that the state had no power to coerce belief; at its greatest the power extended only to the control of actions. But even actions were not absolutely subject to control by the state. Direct proscription of religious actions was sanctioned in *Reynolds*[380] and *Prince*.[381] "In such cases, to make accommodation between the religious action and an exercise of state authority is a particularly delicate task . . . because resolution in favor of the State results in the choice to the individual of either abandoning his religious principle or facing criminal prosecution."[382] The *Braunfeld* case presented no such problem. The Pennsylvania statute did not directly impinge on any religious practice: "the Sunday law simply regulates a secular activity and, as applied to appellants, operates so as to make the practice of their religious beliefs more expensive."[383] Indirect burdens on religion, apparently like indirect burdens on interstate commerce, do not—almost by definition—violate the freedom of religion provision. "To strike down, without the most critical scrutiny, legislation which imposes only an indirect burden on the exercise of religion, *i.e.*, legislation which does not make unlawful the religious practice itself, would radically restrict the operating latitude of the legislature."[384]

Warren then approached the statement of a test not vastly different from that suggested herein:

> If the purpose or effect of a law is to impede the observance of one or all religions or is to discriminate invidiously between religions, that law is constitutionally invalid even though the burden may be characterized as being only indirect. But if the State regulated conduct enacting a general law within its power, the purpose and effect of which is to advance the State's secular goals, the statute is valid despite its indirect burden on religious observance unless the State may accomplish its purpose by means which do not impose such a burden.[385]

Admittedly, the qualifying clause at the end of this quotation is not a necessary ingredient of the standard suggested in this essay. It is in response to the qualification that the Chief Justice was called upon to answer the argument that the State's purposes could be accomplished by exempting those from the operation of the Sunday closing laws who, by reason of their religious obligations, observe some other closing day. His response was that "reason and experience" show that such exemptions undermine the purpose of a day without "the atmosphere of commercial noise and activity."[386] Moreover, it would require inquiry by the state into religious beliefs; it might interfere with the effectuation of the fair employment practices law; it would make enforcement difficult. But the most cogent argument set forth on this score underlines the proposition that the two religion clauses of the first amendment are not separable in their treatment. Mr. Justice Black would seem to be recognizing this proposition when, in each of the cases presented, he asserted that persons who had standing to litigate the "establishment" issue, also, necessarily, had standing to litigate the "freedom" issue. The Chief Justice's recognition comes more obliquely: "To allow only people who rest on a day other than Sunday to keep their businesses open on that day might well provide these people with an economic advantage over their competitors who must remain closed on that day; this might cause the Sunday observers to complain that their religions are being discriminated against."[387] In short, classification of exemption in terms of religious belief raises problems under the freedom and establishment clauses, problems that are not separable. The Supreme Court of Louisiana recognized this as long ago as 1874, when it struck down a conviction of a non-Jew for operating his business on Sunday when Jews were permitted to carry on their business at that time: "Before the constitution, Jews and Gentiles are equal; by the law they must be treated alike, and the ordinance of a City Council which gives to one sect a privilege which it denies to another, violates both the constitution and the law, and is therefore null and void."[388]

Mr. Justice Frankfurter, joined by Mr. Justice Harlan, agreed with the conclusions reached by the Chief Justice in each of the four cases. He filed a separate opinion because he thought it appropriate to do so in a constitutional matter where: "Such expression of differences in view or even in emphasis converging toward the same result makes for the clarity of candor and thereby enhances the authority of the judicial process."[389] One may admire the extensive research and history revealed in this concurring opinion and yet wonder whether its very breadth of coverage will add clarity or confusion for those lawyers and judges called upon to put these materials to further use in the future procession of constitutional litigation.[390] One may wonder, too, whether the advantages to be gained from the separate opinion would have been limited in any way had Mr. Justice Frankfurter joined in the opinion of the Chief Justice in *Gallagher* and *Braunfeld*, at least, in order to provide an opinion for the Court, however slight the danger might be that the plurality opinion should not be considered as authoritative disposition of the issues.[391]

Mr. Justice Frankfurter began with a statement of the "balancing-of-interests" doctrine, with which his opinions in the due process area are so closely associated:

> If the value to society of achieving the object of a particular regulation is demonstrably outweighted by the impediment to which the regulation subjects those whose religious practices are curtailed by it, or if the object sought by the regulation could with equal effect be achieved by alternative means which do not substantially impede those religious practices, the regulation cannot be sustained.[392]

He then denied the separability of the freedom and establishment clauses without accepting their inseparability; for him, they overlap. "In view of the competition among religious creeds, whatever 'establishes' one sect disadvantages another, and vice versa."[393] He also concurred in the Chief Justice's position that the separation clause does more than provide a buttress for the freedom clause. "[P]rotection of unpopular creeds, however, was not to be the full extent of the Amendment's guarantee of freedom from governmental intrusion in matters of faith."[394] In restating this conclusion, he later came closer to stating the theme for which this paper contends and at the same time provided an answer to one of the primary thorny problems of the cases: what is to be done when the secular interests of the state parallel more ancient religious interests of a church:

> The purpose of the Establishment Clause was to assure that the national legislature would not exert its power in the service of any purely religious end; that it would not, as Virginia and virtually all of the Colonies had

done, make of religion, as religion, an object of legislation.

... The Establishment Clause withdrew from the sphere of legitimate legislative concern and competence a specific, but comprehensive, area of human conduct: man's belief or disbelief in the verity of some transcendental idea and man's expression of action of that belief or disbelief. ...

With regulations which have other objectives the Establishment Clause, and the fundamental separationist concept which it expresses are not concerned. ... [O]nce it is determined that a challenged statute is supportable as implementing other substantial interests than the promotion of belief, the guarantee prohibiting religious "establishment" is satisfied.

To ask what interest, what objective, legislation serves, of course, is not to psychoanalyze its legislators, but to examine the necessary effects of what they have enacted. If the primary end achieved by a form of regulation is the affirmation or promotion of religious doctrine—primary, in the sense that all secular ends which it purportedly serves are derivative from, not wholly independent of, the advancement of religion—the regulation is beyond the power of the state. This was the case in *McCollum*. Or if a statute furthers both secular and religious ends by means unnecessary to the effectuation of the secular ends alone—where the same secular ends could equally be attained by means which do not have consequences for promotion of religion—the statute cannot stand.[395]

And, finally, back to the proposition that the establishment clause is more than a supplement to the freedom clause: "the constitutional prohibition of religious establishment is a provision of more comprehensive availability than the guarantee of free exercise, insofar as both give content to the prohibited fusion of church and state."[396] From this he drew the somewhat doubtful conclusion that because they are different in their nature, they are separable in their application.

At this point in his opinion came the extensive historical proof of the religious origins of the observance of Sunday by abstention from matters of worldly affairs, both in England and the United States, and an equally lengthy showing of the development of the secular reasons for a day of recreation in each week, with the conclusion, also reached by the Chief Justice, that the secular became dominant over the religious. By this evidence he demonstrated that the application of the principles that he had previously stated required the validation of the Sunday closing laws as consonant with the dictates of the establishment clause.

In balancing the interests of the state in securing the secular objectives of the Sunday closing laws against the economic injury done to Orthodox Jews who are compelled by religious reasons to close on Saturday as well, he concluded that the state's choice was a reasonable one for reasons not unlike those put forth in the Warren opinions. Nor was he particularly troubled by the other due process and equal protection arguments asserted; but, unlike Mr. Justice Harlan, he would give the plaintiffs in the *Braunfeld* case an opportunity to prove the allegations in their complaint that the "Pennsylvania Sunday retail sales act is irrational and arbitrary."[397]

Mr. Justice Douglas was alone in dissenting from the judgments in all four cases. He would pose the problem differently from the others. "The question is whether a State can impose criminal sanctions on those who, unlike the Christian majority that makes up our society, worship on a different day or do not share the religious scruples of the majority."[398] For him, the author of *Zorach*,[399] both the separation and the freedom clauses establish absolutes that cannot be qualified. "With that as my starting point I do not see how a State can make protesting citizens refrain from doing innocent acts on Sunday because the doing of those acts offends sentiments of their Christian neighbors."[400] That Sunday closing is religious in its objectives was clear to him: "Sunday is a word heavily overlaid with connotations and traditions deriving from the Christian roots of our civilization that color all judgments concerning it. This is what the philosophers call 'word magic.' "[401] "We have then in each of the four cases Sunday laws that find their source in Exodus, that were brought here by the Virginians and by the Puritans, and that are today maintained, construed, and justified because they respect the views of our dominant religious groups and provide a needed day of rest."[402]

In addition to the absolute commands of the two religion clauses, Mr. Justice Douglas recognized their inseparable nature: "The reverse side of an 'establishment' is a burden on the 'free exercise' of religion."[403] He did not, however, note that the reverse side of "free exercise" might be "establishment." But his principal problem derived not from this conjunction, but rather from his notion of the absolute nature of the first amendment commands. He can distinguish *Reynolds* and *Prince*: "None of the acts involved here implicates minors. None of the actions made constitutionally criminal today involves the doing of any act that any society has deemed to be immoral."[404] Are the absolutes of the first amendment then qualified where minors are involved or where the acts involved are accepted by some societies as "immoral"? Mr. Justice Douglas did not answer the question; it is doubtful whether he can in such a way as to reconcile on principle the cases that he can reconcile on the facts.

Essentially, Mr. Justice Douglas seemed to believe that, however well covered up by proffered secular reasons, the basic function of the Sunday closing laws was to assure the Christian churches conformity with their dictate that Sunday be observed as a day of rest and prayer. It is here that his quarrel with the majority really lay, for if they accepted his characterization of the function of the closing laws, they too would find them unconstitutional both in terms of establishment and in terms of freedom. The Douglas conclusion need not rest on the absolutism of construction that he espouses. As stated, his difference with the majority in this case was really to be found elsewhere.

Treating the problem of establishment and freedom the way he did, Mr. Justice Douglas did not have to answer that difficult problem that faced the other minority of two Justices, Brennan and Stewart, who found no establishment but did find interference with the freedom of religion of Orthodox Jews who wanted to open their stores on Sunday because they had kept them closed on Saturday.

The opinion written by Mr. Justice Brennan in the *Braunfeld* case served for all four cases. Sunday laws are not promulgated for religious purposes but rather for secular ones. The only issue, therefore, was whether the Constitution required an exemption for those whose religious beliefs called upon them to close on a day other than Sunday. None of the reasons offered by the Chief Justice or by Mr. Justice Frankfurter proved persuasive that the difficulties that would result from such exemption were sufficiently large so as to warrant this hardship on religious minorities. After all, "a majority—21—of the 34 States which have general Sunday regulations have exemptions of this kind."[405] Brennan and Stewart were apparently not concerned with the problem whether an exemption from a validly promulgated police regulation framed in terms of religious belief constituted a violation of the "establishment clause."[406]

Of the two hundred pages of opinions, it might be noted that only those few contributed by Justices Brennan and Stewart are inconsistent with the thesis offered herein. This is not to suggest that the Court had adopted the views tendered here, but only that in the search for the appropriate neutral principles, the Sunday closing law cases offer no barrier to the appropriate rationale.

12

THE NOTARY'S OATH

Unanimity was restored to the Court's views on church and state problems when it decided that Maryland could not constitutionally require an office holder to swear to his belief in God before being permitted to enter upon his office. American politics being what it is, a devotion to God, to country, and to mother is usually readily professed by every actual and potential office holder. There is hoary tradition for this: George Washington added the words "so help me God" to his presidential oath and every successor has done the same. The unlikely case that came to the Court involved only the office of notary public. In *Torcaso v. Watkins*,[407] the appellant had been appointed to that high office by the Governor of Maryland but had been barred from exercising the perquisites of office because of his refusal to swear to a belief in God. The Maryland constitution had barred all religious tests for office except this one.[408] The Maryland courts upheld the right of the State to demand such an oath against Torcaso's contentions that such a requirement violated the first and fourteenth amendments.[409]

Mr. Justice Black, on behalf of six of his brethren, wrote the opinion for the Court reversing the judgment of the Maryland high court. Justices Frankfurter and Harlan concurred in the result. Black quickly disposed of the notion on which the Maryland courts had based their conclusions, that *Zorach* had repudiated the grounds of decision stated in *Everson*. Equally deficient was the argument that a person could not be compelled to profess his beliefs, but the granting of an office could be conditioned on such profession since there was no right to hold office. The rationale was quickly and easily stated:

Nothing decided or written in *Zorach* lends support to the idea that the Court there intended to open up the way for government, state or federal, to restore the historically and constitutionally discredited policy of probing religious beliefs by test oaths or limiting public offices to persons who

107

have, or perhaps more properly profess to have, a belief in some particular kind of religious concept.

We repeat and again reaffirm that neither a State nor the Federal Government can constitutionally force a person "to profess a belief or disbelief in any religion." Neither can constitutionally pass laws nor impose requirements which aid all religions as against non-believers, and neither can aid those religions based on a belief in the existence of God as against those religions founded on different beliefs. . . . The fact . . . that a person is not compelled to hold public office cannot possibly be an excuse for barring him from office by state-imposed criteria forbidden by the Constitution.[410]

The Court did not bother to distinguish *Davis v. Beason*[411] and it left the dictum of *Church of the Holy Trinity*[412] unnoticed, thus paying it its due regard.

PART THREE

Conclusion

13

CONCLUSION

One need not turn back many pages of history to recognize the importance and delicacy of the problems presented by the relation of religion to government. The many faces of these issues have been making recent newspaper headlines in profusion. Some of them are beyond judicial cognizance: for example, those so well recorded in Mr. White's book on the 1960 presidential election.[413] There are others that may or may not become appropriate subjects for judicial scrutiny, such as the continuing question whether the national government can contribute financially to parochial education, directly or indirectly. (Anyone suggesting that the answer, as a matter of constitutional law, is clear one way or the other is either deluding or deluded.) Fortunately, the church-state problems in this country have not been those of countries like Spain and Colombia, where intolerance—indeed, persecution—is a policy of state and church in combination. But these countries provide ample contemporary evidence of the wisdom of the framers of the first amendment in their objectives of keeping the church free from domination by government and the state free from alliance with religion. There is little quarrel, today, about the goals to be achieved by the religion clauses of the first amendment. The problem that has bemused and confused the Court has been that of stating appropriate principles to serve as means to agreed-upon ends. But there has been no consistency in the judicial opinions of the Court. The seeming simplicity of the "absolutist" construction of the first amendment is only too patently disingenuous. The method of weighing constitutional objectives in order to choose among them affords no guidance for further action, except on what Holmes called a "pots and pans" basis. The action-belief dichotomy is obviously inadequate to attainment of the stated goals of the religion clauses.

This paper has stated and examined, in the context of the Court's opinions, a principle believed to be appropriate to the first amendment objectives.

The principle tendered is a simple one. The freedom and separation clauses should be read as stating a single precept: that government cannot utilize religion as a standard for action or inaction because these clauses, read together as they should be, prohibit classification in terms of religion either to confer a benefit or to impose a burden. This test is meant to provide a starting point for the solution to problems brought before the Court, not a mechanical answer to them. Perhaps such a search for rules of decision is futile or undesirable. Certainly the recent plea for "neutral principles" of constitutional adjudication[414] has not met with uniform acclaim.[415] Only if equality and certainty are still fundamental objectives of our legal structure do such principles have a function to serve. And perhaps this notion of law is outdated in the society in which we live. But no apologies are offered for the belief that democratic society cannot survive if these elements of the rule of law are rejected.

NOTES

1 MCCLOSKEY, THE AMERICAN SUPREME COURT 251 (1960).

2 MURRAY, WE HOLD THESE TRUTHS 58 (1960).

3 *Id.*, at pp. 58-59.

4 *Cf.* 4 JORDAN, THE DEVELOPMENT OF RELIGIOUS TOLERATION IN ENGLAND 475 (1940): "It is likewise apparent that religious indifference became for the first time widespread in England during the last decade of the revolutionary era. This most powerful dissolvent of religious zeal was to be a factor of very great importance in the development of religious toleration. The indifferent man is tolerant of all religions because he lends his devotion to none."

5 *Cf. id.* at 482: "We may suggest, furthermore, that the convincing fact of religious diversity imposed a spiritual necessity of religious liberty quite as persuasively as it suggested the political necessity for the legal toleration of orderly dissent."

6 *Cf.* TAWNEY, RELIGION AND THE RISE OF CAPITALISM 205 (1937 ed.): "A many-sided business community could escape constant friction and obstruction only if it were free to absorb elements drawn from a multitude of different sources, and if each of these elements were free to pursue its own way of life, and—in that age the same thing—to practice its own religion."

7 JORDAN, *op. cit. supra* note 4, at 476-77.

8 See, *e.g.*, MILLER, ROGER WILLIAMS (1953); ERNST, THE POLITICAL THOUGHT OF ROGER WILLIAMS (1929).

9 2 BRYCE, THE AMERICAN COMMONWEALTH 698 (3d ed. 1903).

10 *Cf.* Gomillion v. Lightfoot, 364 U.S. 339, 347 (1960): "While in form this is merely an act redefining metes and bounds, if the allegations are established, the inescapable human effect of this essay in geometry and geography is to despoil colored citizens, and only colored citizens, of their theretofore enjoyed voting rights."

11 HAYEK, THE CONSTITUTION OF LIBERTY 209 (1960).

12 See LEVI, AN INTRODUCTION TO LEGAL REASONING 41-72 (1948).

13 For earlier consideration of problems of church and state by the Court, see, *e.g.*, Vidal v. Girard's Executors, 43 U.S. (2 How.) 127 (1844); Permoli v. Municipality # 1 of New Orleans, 44 U.S. (3 How.) 589 (1845). See also cases cited note 344 *infra*.

14 98 U.S. 145 (1878).

113

[15] *Id.* at 164.

[16] BRYCE, *op. cit. supra* note 9, at 699.

[17] 98 U.S. at 162.

[18] *Ibid.*

[19] Mr. Justice Field took exception only to the admissibility of testimony given at an earlier trial on a different indictment. *Id.* at 168.

[20] *Id.* at 164.

[21] *Id.* at 166.

[22] "Professor Lieber says, polygamy leads to the patriarchal principle, and which, when applied to large communities, fetters the people in stationary despotism, while that principle cannot long exist in connection with monogamy. . . . but there cannot be a doubt that, unless restricted by some form of constitution, it is within the legitimate scope of the power of every civil government to determine whether polygamy or monogamy shall be the law of social life under its dominion." *Ibid.* Mr. Chief Justice Waite had previously established the criminal nature of polygamy at common law. *Id.* at 164–65.

[23] "Waite himself spoke of this decision as his 'sermon.' 'I send you enclosed my sermon on the religion of polygamy. * * * I hope you will not find it poisoned with heterodoxy.' " TRIMBLE, CHIEF JUSTICE WAITE 244 n.18 (1938).

[24] The principles announced in the *Reynolds* case were reaffirmed by the Court as recently as the 1946 Term, in Cleveland v. United States, 329 U.S. 14 (1946), where the Court sustained the conviction under the Mann Act of Mormon fundamentalists who took their "plural wives" across state lines. Mr. Justice Douglas, speaking for the Court, said: "It is also urged that the requisite criminal intent was lacking since petitioners were motivated by a religious belief. That defense claims too much. If upheld, it would place beyond the law any act done under claim of religious sanction. But it has long been held that the fact that polygamy is supported by a religious creed affords no defense in a prosecution for bigamy." 329 U.S. at 20.

[25] At this distance in time it is somewhat difficult to realize the hatred for the Mormons in this country during the second half of the nineteenth century. It was by no means confined to the areas in which they settled. For the literature on this subject, see Hill, *The Historiography of Mormonism,* 28 CHURCH HISTORY 418 (1959). For one of the few balanced studies of the Mormons in the United States, see O'DEA, THE MORMONS (1957).

[26] 133 U.S. 333 (1890).

[27] *Id.* at 334. (Emphasis added.)

[28] *Id.* at 337.

[29] *Id.* at 338.

[30] *Id.* at 339–40.

[31] 118 U.S. 356 (1886).

[32] 133 U.S. at 341–42.

[33] *Id.* at 342–43.

[34] *Id.* at 345.

[35] "It is unnecessary here to refer to the past history of the sect, to their defiance of the government authorities, to their attempt to establish an independent community, to their efforts to drive from the territory all who were not connected with them in communion and sympathy. The tale is one of patience on the part of the American government and people, and of contempt of authority and resistance to law on the part of the Mormons. Whatever persecutions they may have suffered in the early part of their history, in Missouri and

Illinois, they have no excuse for their persistent defiance of law under the government of the United States.

"One pretence for this obstinate course is, that their belief in the practice of polygamy, or in the right to indulge in it, is a religious belief, and, therefore, under the protection of the constitutional guaranty of religious freedom. This is altogether a sophistical plea. No doubt the Thugs of India imagined that their belief in the right of assassination was a religious belief; but their thinking so did not make it so. The practice of suttee by the Hindu widows may have sprung from a supposed religious conviction. The offering of human sacrifice by our own ancestors in Britain was no doubt sanctioned by an equally conscientious impulse. But no one, on that account, would hesitate to brand these practices, now, as crimes against society, and obnoxious to condemnation and punishment by the civil authority." Bradley, J., in Mormon Church v. United States, 136 U.S. 1, 49–50 (1890). In that case, in which the Court sanctioned the confiscation of the property of the Mormon Church, over the dissents of Fuller, Field, and Lamar, the parties apparently did not raise the issue of the religion clauses of the first amendment. See also Snow v. United States, 118 U.S. 346 (1886); Clawson v. United States, 114 U.S. 477 (1885); Murphy v. Ramsey, 114 U.S. 15 (1885); Cannon v. United States, 116 U.S. 55 (1885); Miles v. United States, 103 U.S. 304 (1881). Each of these involved cases in which there were serious questions of the infringement of rights under the first amendment, but in none of them did counsel present the problems for resolution by the Court. They demonstrate the judicial climate in which the Mormons were prosecuted.

36 364 U.S. 339 (1960). See note 10 *supra.*

37 *Cf.* Torasco v. Watkins, 367 U.S. 488 (1961), discussed *infra,* at pp. 107-108.

38 143 U.S. 457, 471 (1892).

39 BRYCE, *op. cit. supra* note 9, at 701.

40 143 U.S. 457 (1892).

41 *Id.* at 465.

42 *Ibid.*

43 "I, A.B., do profess faith in God the Father, and in Jesus Christ His only Son, and in the Holy Ghost, one God, blessed for evermore; and I do acknowledge the Holy Scriptures of the Old and New Testament to be given by divine inspiration." Quoted, *id.* at 469–70.

44 8 Johns. 290 (N.Y. 1811), quoted, 143 U.S. at 470–71.

45 268 U.S. 510 (1925).

46 259 U.S. 20 (1922).

47 236 U.S. 1 (1915).

48 262 U.S. 390 (1923).

49 268 U.S. at 535.

50 *Id.* at 535–36.

51 The procedural holding of the case, too, is now doubtful at best. In the Sunday closing law cases, standing was sought by business enterprises to assert the rights to freedom of religion of their customers to make purchases on Sunday. In the principal opinion, the Court said: "Since the general rule is that 'a litigant may only assert his own constitutional rights or immunities,' . . . we hold that appellants have no standing to raise this contention. . . . Furthermore, since appellants do not specifically allege that the statutes infringe upon the religious beliefs of the department store's present or prospective patrons, we have no occasion here to consider the standing question of *Pierce* v. *Society of Sisters*. . . . Those persons whose religious rights are allegedly impaired by the statutes are not without effective ways to assert these rights." McGowan v. Maryland, 366 U.S. 420, 429–30 (1961).

52 281 U.S. 370 (1930).

53 Record, p. 4.

54 *Id.* at 6.

55 *Ibid.*

56 *Id.* at 13.

57 *Id.* at 16. This position differs from that taken in this paper. I believe that a classification in terms of public and non-public schools would be valid. See the discussion of the *Everson* case at pp. 80-85 *infra*.

58 Frothingham v. Mellon, 262 U.S. 447 (1923).

59 Record, p. 20.

60 The governing opinion was written in the companion case of Borden v. Louisiana State Board of Educ., 168 La. 1006 (1929). The opinion in the *Cochran* case, incorporating the *Borden* case by reference, is found at 168 La. 1030 (1929).

61 168 La. at 1019.

62 *Id.* at 1027.

63 281 U.S. at 374–75.

64 *Id.* at 375.

65 Statement in Support of Motion to Dismiss for Want of Jurisdiction, p. 13.

66 Brief on Behalf of Appellees, p. 30.

67 See pp. 32-34 *infra*.

68 175 U.S. 291 (1899).

69 Frothingham v. Mellon, 262 U.S. 447 (1923).

70 175 U.S. at 295.

71 *Id.* at 297.

72 *Id.* at 298.

73 Brown v. Board of Educ., 347 U.S. 483 (1954).

74 Quick Bear v. Leupp, 210 U.S. 50 (1908). But *cf.* Pennsylvania v. Board of Directors, 353 U.S. 230 (1957), holding that trustees of a college who were members of a state agency could not abide by the trust requirement limiting attendance at the college to white students.

75 284 U.S. 573 (1931).

76 342 U.S. 429 (1952).

77 5 N.J. 435, 75 A.2d 880 (1950).

78 262 U.S. 447 (1923).

79 342 U.S. at 433.

80 Everson v. Board of Educ., 330 U.S. 1 (1947). See pp. 80-85 *infra*.

81 342 U.S. at 434.

82 McCollum v. Board of Educ., 333 U.S. 203 (1948); Zorach v. Clauson, 343 U.S. 306 (1952). See pp. 86-89 *infra*.

83 See pp. 32-34 *supra*.

84 See pp. 28-31 *supra*.

85 239 U.S. 175 (1915). See notes 102 and 103 *infra*.

86 325 U.S. 561 (1945). See pp. 47-49 *supra*.

87 School Dist. of Abington Township v. Schempp, 364 U.S. 298 (1960).

88 Act of May 18, 1917, ch. 15, § 4, 40 Stat. 78 (1919).

89 245 U.S. 366 (1918).

90 *Id.* at 389–90.

91 Hamilton v. Regents, 293 U.S. 245, 252 (1934).

92 *Id.* at 252.

93 *Id.* at 252–53; Record, p. 4.

94 Hamilton v. Regents of the Univ. of California, 219 Cal. 663, 664, 28 P.2d 355 (1934).

95 Coale v. Pearson, 290 U.S. 597 (1933).

96 University of Maryland v. Coale, 165 Md. 224, 167 Atl. 54 (1933).

97 283 U.S. 605, 623–24 (1931). "The conscientious objector is relieved from the obligation to bear arms in obedience to no constitutional provision, express or implied; but because, and only because, it has accorded with the policy of Congress thus to relieve him. . . . The privilege of the . . . conscientious objector to avoid bearing arms comes, not from the Constitution, but from the acts of Congress. That body may grant or withhold the exemption as in its wisdom it sees fit; and, if it be withheld, the . . . conscientious objector cannot successfully assert the privilege. No other conclusion is compatible with the well-nigh limitless extent of the war powers . . . which include, by necessary implication, the power, in the last extremity, to compel the armed service of any citizen in the land, without regard to his objections or his views in respect of the justice or morality of the particular war or of war in general." As quoted, 165 Md. at 233, 167 Atl. at 57.

98 197 U.S. 11 (1905). "And yet he may be compelled, by force if need be, against his will and without regard to his personal wishes or his peculiar interests, or even his religious or political convictions, to take his place in the ranks of the army of his country, and risk the chance of being shot down in its defense." As quoted, 165 Md. at 233, 167 Atl. at 57.

99 Equitable Life Assur. Soc'y v. Brown, 187 U.S. 308, 311 (1902); Roe v. Kansas, 278 U.S. 191 (1929) (frivolous); American Baseball Club v. Philadelphia, 290 U.S. 595 (1933).

100 191 U.S. 207 (1903).

101 *Id.* at 222–23.

102 239 U.S. 175 (1915).

103 *Id.* at 186–87. "There seems to have been no question raised as to the right of Heim to maintain the suit, although he is not one of the contractors nor a laborer of the excluded nationality or citizenship. The Appellate Division felt that there might be objection to the right, under the holding of a cited case. The Court of Appeals, however, made no comment, and we must—certainly may—assume that Heim had a right of suit; and, so assuming, we pass to the merits."

104 287 U.S. 251, 275–76 (1932).

105 237 U.S. 589 (1915)

106 293 U.S. at 258.

107 *Id.* at 264.

108 *Id.* at 266.

109 *Id.* at 268.

110 Cited *id.* at 265.

111 See p. 22 *supra.*

112 310 U.S. 586 (1940).

113 *Id.* at 594–95.

114 Leoles v. Landers, 302 U.S. 656 (1937); Hering v. State Board of Educ., 303 U.S. 624 (1938).

115 Johnson v. Deerfield, 306 U.S. 621 (1939).

116 Gabrielli v. Knickerbocker, 306 U.S. 621 (1939).

117 People v. Sandstrom, 279 N.Y. 523 (1939).

118 Minersville School Dist. v. Gobitis, 108 F.2d 683 (3d Cir. 1939).

119 Record, p. 6, 310 U.S. 586 (1940).

120 *Id.,* p. 7. The Court added the third verse as the basis for their complaint, apparently in reliance on the brief rather than the complaint.

121 Gobitis v. Minersville School Dist., 21 F. Supp. 581, 585–86 (E.D. Pa. 1937).

122 Gobitis v. Minersville School Dist., 24 F. Supp. 271, 273 (E.D. Pa. 1938).

123 Minersville School Dist. v. Gobitis, 108 F.2d 683 (3d Cir. 1939). This is an opinion, not untypical of this judge, that must be read to be appreciated. It cannot be adequately summarized.

124 *Id.* at 692.

125 Brief for Petitioners, pp. 27–32, 310 U.S. 586 (1940).

126 Respondents' Brief, *passim.*

127 Brief for American Civil Liberties Union as Amicus Curiae, p. 20.

128 *Id.* at 27. *Cf.* Pennsylvania v. Nelson, 350 U.S. 497 (1956).

129 Brief of the Committee on the Bill of Rights, of the American Bar Association as Friends of the Court, p. 37. The Committee, at the time the brief was filed, consisted of Douglas Arant, Zechariah Chafee, Jr., Grenville Clark, Osmer C. Fitts, Lloyd K. Garrison, George I. Haight, Monte M. Lemann, Ross L. Malone, Jr., Burton W. Musser, Joseph A. Padway, and Charles P. Taft. *Id.* at 43.

130 310 U.S. at 598.

131 *Id.* at 602.

132 *Id.* at 605.

133 319 U.S. 624 (1943).

134 *Id.* at 634–36.

135 See p. 44 *supra.*

136 319 U.S. at 642.

137 *Id.* at 643.

138 *Id.* at 653.

139 *Id.* at 654.

140 *Id.* at 658.

141 A footnote was added to the *Barnette* case by Taylor v. Mississippi, 319 U.S. 583 (1943), upsetting a conviction by a Mississippi court for teaching resistance to the compulsory flag-salute regulation. Mr. Justice Roberts wrote for a unanimous Court. It is of interest

that he rested on freedom of religion as the ground for decision, and apparently regarded that as the basis for the *Barnette* judgment: "[T]he court has decided that a state may not enforce a regulation requiring children in the public schools to salute the national emblem. The statute here in question seeks to punish as a criminal one who teaches resistance to governmental compulsion to salute. If the Fourteenth Amendment bans enforcement of the school regulation, *a fortiori* it prohibits the imposition of punishment for urging and advising that, on religious grounds, citizens refrain from saluting the flag. If the state cannot constrain one to violate his conscientious religious conviction by saluting the national emblem, then certainly it cannot punish him for imparting his views on the subject to his fellows and exhorting them to accept those views." *Id.* at 588–89.

142 See generally COMMAGER, MAJORITY RULE AND MINORITY RIGHTS (1943), for an historian's evaluation of the problem.

143 325 U.S. 561 (1945). *Cf. In re* Anastaplo, 366 U.S. 82 (1961); Konigsberg v. State Bar of California, 366 U.S. 36 (1961).

144 325 U.S. at 564 n.4.

145 An example makes the point. Summers was asked about the reading that had led him to his conclusion of conscientious objection. Among other readings he referred to some by Reinhold Niebuhr. His inquisitor responded: "He is a Communist? A. No. He is a minister. Q. Didn't you know he was a Communist? A. I never heard of it—not Neber [sic]. Q. Did you read any of his books on Russia? A. No, sir. I have not. Q. Do you know whether he wrote about Russia or not? A. I do not know of anything if he did." Record, p. 26.

146 See, *e.g.*, Record at pp. 6, 18, 46.

147 The Illinois Supreme Court held that there was no case or controversy presented by the application for admission.

148 325 U.S. at 573. It is equally irrelevant that those decisions have since been overruled by the Supreme Court. Girouard v. United States, 328 U.S. 61 (1946).

149 United States v. Schwimmer, 279 U.S. 644 (1929).

150 United States v. Macintosh, 283 U.S. 605 (1931).

151 325 U.S. at 577.

152 283 U.S. at 627.

153 325 U.S. at 578.

154 Lovell v. City of Griffin, 303 U.S. 444 (1938).

155 Coleman v. City of Griffin, 55 Ga. App. 123 (1936). It held that other grounds for complaint under the fourteenth amendment were not specifically raised.

156 Coleman v. City of Griffin, 302 U.S. 636 (1937).

157 303 U.S. at 450.

158 *Id.* at 451.

159 Schneider v. State, 308 U.S. 147 (1939).

160 *Id.* at 164.

161 *Id.* at 165. "Conceding that fraudulent appeals may be made in the name of charity and religion, we hold a municipality cannot, for this reason, require all who wish to disseminate ideas to present them first to police authorities for their consideration and approval, with a discretion in the police to say some ideas may, while others may not, be carried to the homes of citizens; some persons may, while others may not, disseminate information from house to house. Frauds may be denounced as offenses and punished by law. Trespasses may similarly be forbidden. If it is said that these means are less efficient and convenient than bestowal of power on police authorities to decide what information may be dissemi-

nated from house to house, and who may impart the information, the answer is that considerations of this sort do not empower a municipality to abridge freedom of speech and press." *Id.* at 164.

162 310 U.S. 296 (1940).

163 See Finding of Fact No. 9, Record, p. 19; Finding of Fact No. 21, Record, p. 21.

164 See Record, pp. 40–52.

165 CONN. GEN. STATS. § 6294 (1930), as amended by § 860(d) of Connecticut Public Act of 1937.

166 State v. Cantwell, 126 Conn. 1, 8 A.2d 533 (1939).

167 *Id.* at 4–5, 8 A.2d at 536.

168 *Id.* at 7, 8 A.2d at 537.

169 *Id.* at 6, 8 A.2d at 537.

170 310 U.S. at 305.

171 *Id.* at 306–07.

172 *Id.* at 310.

173 *Id.* at 311 n.10.

174 *Id.* at 311.

175 312 U.S. 569 (1941).

176 *Id.* at 577.

177 *Id.* at 578.

178 *Ibid.*

179 315 U.S. 568 (1942).

180 N.H. PUB. LAWS ch. 378, § 2 (1926).

181 315 U.S. at 569.

182 *Id.* at 571.

183 "There are certain well-defined and narrowly limited classes of speech, the prevention and punishment of which have never been thought to raise any Constitutional problem. These include the lewd and obscene, the profane, the libelous, and the insulting or 'fighting' words—those which by their very utterance inflict injury or tend to incite an immediate breach of the peace. It has been well observed that such utterances are no essential part of any exposition of ideas, and are of such slight social value as a step to truth that any benefit that may be derived from them is clearly outweighed by the social interest in order and morality." *Id.* at 571–72. See Kalven, *The Metaphysics of the Law of Obscenity*, 1960 SUP. CT. REV. 1, for other problems of the "two-level" theory of free speech.

184 318 U.S. 413 (1943).

185 See pp. 50-51 *supra.*

186 318 U.S. at 416–17.

187 See LEVI, AN INTRODUCTION TO LEGAL REASONING (1948).

188 318 U.S. at 417.

189 318 U.S. 418 (1943).

190 *Id.* at 422.

191 319 U.S. 105 (1943).

192 316 U.S. 584 (1942).

193 *Id.* at 593–94.

194 *Id.* at 595.

195 *Id.* at 596–97.

196 *Id.* at 598.

197 *Id.* at 598–99.

198 *Id.* at 620–21.

199 *Id.* at 621.

200 *Id.* at 623–24.

201 See pp. 41-47 *supra.*

202 317 U.S. 589–90 (1942).

203 318 U.S. 739 (1943).

204 319 U.S. 141 (1943).

205 319 U.S. 157 (1943).

206 319 U.S. at 108–09.

207 Cox v. New Hampshire, 312 U.S. 569, 578 (1941).

208 See pp. 86-90 *infra.*

209 319 U.S. at 115.

210 *Id.* at 116.

211 *Id.* at 139–40.

212 319 U.S. at 142.

213 *Id.* at 141–42.

214 *Id.* at 147.

215 "For this reason, and wholly aside from any other possible defects, on which we do not pass but which are suggested in other opinions filed in this case, we conclude that the ordinance is invalid because in conflict with the freedom of speech and press." *Id.* at 149.

216 *Id.* at 150.

217 *Id.* at 151–52.

218 *Id.* at 154.

219 *Id.* at 179.

220 321 U.S. 158 (1944).

221 *Id.* at 174.

222 *Id.* at 177–78.

223 321 U.S. 573 (1944).

224 *Id.* at 577–78.

225 *Id.* at 578–79.

226 See *id.* at 582 n.2.

227 *Id.* at 580–83.

228 See, *e.g.*, Martin v. City of Struthers, 319 U.S. 141, 147 (1943).

229 326 U.S. 501 (1946).

230 ALA. CODE tit. 14, § 426 (1940).

231 326 U.S. at 502.

232 *Id.* at 504–05.

233 *Id.* at 505.

234 *Id.* at 508.

235 *Id.* at 509.

236 *Id.* at 512.

237 326 U.S. 517 (1946).

238 *Id.* at 520.

239 334 U.S. 558 (1948).

240 *Id.* at 559; see Brief for Appellant, pp. 19–24.

241 334 U.S. at 559–60.

242 *Id.* at 561.

243 *Ibid.*

244 *Id.* at 562.

245 *Id.* at 569–70.

246 336 U.S. 77 (1949).

247 340 U.S. 268 (1951).

248 *Id.* at 272.

249 340 U.S. 290 (1951).

250 *Id.* at 292.

251 *Id.* at 296.

252 *Id.* at 293.

253 340 U.S. 315 (1951).

254 *Id.* at 286.

255 *Id.* at 309.

256 345 U.S. 67 (1953).

257 *Id.* at 69.

258 345 U.S. 395 (1953).

259 *Id.* at 405–07.

260 322 U.S. 78 (1944).

261 Record, p. 2.

262 Petition for Certiorari, pp. 4–5.

263 Brief for Respondents, p. 53.

264 *Id.* at 54, 55.

265 As quoted at page 59 of Respondents' Brief: "Whosoever shall be saved; before all things it is necessary that he hold the Catholic faith; which faith except every one do keep whole and undefiled; without doubt he shall perish everlastingly. * * * This is the Catholic faith; which except a man believe faithfully (truly and firmly), he cannot be saved."

266 Mark 16:16, as quoted *ibid.*

267 *Id.* at 69.

268 *Id.* at 77.

269 *Ibid.*

270 *Ibid.*

271 *Id.* at 79–80.

272 *Id.* at 82.

273 *Id.* at 83.

274 322 U.S. at 81–82.

275 *Id.* at 85–86.

276 *Id.* at 87.

277 The convictions were ultimately upset because women had been systematically excluded from the jury. Ballard v. United States, 329 U.S. 187 (1946).

278 322 U.S. at 89–90.

279 *Id.* at 92–95.

280 330 U.S. 1 (1947).

281 N.J. Rev. Stat. § 18:14–8 (1942).

282 Statement as to Jurisdiction, p. 2.

283 330 U.S. at 7.

284 *Id.* at 15–16.

285 *Id.* at 16. (All italicized in original.)

286 *Id.* at 18.

287 *Id.* at 4 n.2.

288 *Id.* at 19.

289 *Id.* at 21.

290 *Ibid.*

291 *Id.* at 24.

292 *Ibid.*

293 *Ibid.*

294 *Id.* at 25.

295 *Id.* at 33.

296 *Id.* at 52–53.

297 *Id.* at 56.

298 *Id.* at 58.

299 *Id.* at 62.

300 Brown v. Board of Educ., 347 U.S. 483, 493, 494 (1954).

301 333 U.S. 203 (1948).

302 343 U.S. 306 (1952).

303 333 U.S. at 209–10.

304 *Id.* at 212.

305 *Id.* at 227–28.

306 *Id.* at 235, 237.

307 *Id.* at 256.

308 See, *e.g.*, *Religion and the State—A Symposium*, 14 LAW & CONTEMP. PROB. 1 (1949).

309 343 U.S. at 315.

310 *Id.* at 316.

311 *Id.* at 317.

312 *Id.* at 320.

313 *Id.* at 323–24.

314 *Id.* at 324.

315 *Id.* at 325.

316 Kreshik v. Saint Nicholas Cathedral, 363 U.S. 190 (1960).

317 Kedroff v. Saint Nicholas Cathedral, 344 U.S. 94, 126 (1952).

318 See, *e.g.*, ANDERSON, PEOPLE CHURCH, AND STATE IN MODERN RUSSIA (1944); BOL-SHAKOFF, CHRISTIAN CHURCH AND SOVIET STATE (1942); BOLSHAKOFF, THE FOREIGN MIS-SIONS OF THE RUSSIAN ORTHODOX CHURCH (1943); CASEY, RELIGION IN RUSSIA (1946); CURTISS, CHURCH AND STATE IN RUSSIA (1940); DANZAS, THE RUSSIAN CHURCH (1936); EMHARDT, RELIGION IN SOVIET RUSSIA (1929); FEDOTOFF, THE RUSSIAN CHURCH SINCE THE REVOLUTION (1928); FORTESCUE, ORTHODOX EASTERN CHURCH (1916); FRENCH, THE EAST-ERN ORTHODOX CHURCH (1951); SPINKA, THE CHURCH AND THE RUSSIAN REVOLUTION (1927); TIMASHEFF, RELIGION IN SOVIET RUSSIA 1917–1942 (1942); ZERNOV, THE RUSSIANS AND THEIR CHURCH (1945).

319 The same record was used in both the *Kreshik* and *Kedroff* cases.

320 Record, p. 177.

321 See 344 U.S. at 103 n.8.

322 See *id.* at 104 n.9.

323 *Id.* at 97–99.

324 Saint Nicholas Cathedral v. Kedroff, 302 N.Y. 1, 96 N.E.2d 56 (1959).

325 344 U.S. at 108–09.

326 80 U.S. (13 Wall.) 679 (1871).

327 Quoted from 80 U.S. (13 Wall.) at 727, in 344 U.S. at 113.

328 344 U.S. at 120–21.

329 *Id.* at 120.

330 *Id.* at 105–06.

331 See text accompanying note 320 *supra*.

332 344 U.S. at 106.

333 *Id.* at 122.

334 *Id.* at 125.

335 *Id.* at 121.

336 *Id.* at 130.

337 See, *e.g.*, Howe, *The Constitutional Question*, in RELIGION AND THE FREE SOCIETY 54–55 (1958).

338 Saint Nicholas Cathedral v. Kreshik, 7 N.Y.2d 191, 181 N.Y.S.2d 677 (1959).

339 363 U.S. at 190.

340 See text accompanying note 333 *supra*.

341 There was no contest of the fact that one of the commands of the Russian church as administered from Moscow to the American communicants was "to abstain 'from political activities against the U.S.S.R.' " 344 U.S. at 105.

342 McGowan v. Maryland, 366 U.S. 420 (1961); Gallagher v. Crown Kosher Super Market, 366 U.S. 617 (1961); Braunfeld v. Brown, 366 U.S. 599 (1961); Two Guys from Harrison-Allentown, Inc. v. McGinley, 366 U.S. 582 (1961).

343 See, *e.g.*, Friedman v. New York, 341 U.S. 907 (1951); McGee v. North Carolina, 346 U.S. 802 (1953); Gundaker Central Motors, Inc. v. Gassert, 354 U.S. 933 (1957); Grochowiak v. Pennsylvania, 358 U.S. 47 (1958); Ullner v. Ohio, 358 U.S. 131 (1958); Kidd v. Ohio, 358 U.S. 132 (1958).

344 In addition to the cases discussed in the text there were many others not decided with relevance to the constitutional problems. The first case reported in the *United States Reports* on this subject was a case decided not by the Supreme Court of the United States but by the Supreme Court of Pennsylvania. The case in full: "In this case (which was tried on Saturday, the 5th of April), the defendant offered Jonas Phillips, a Jew, as a witness; but he refused to be sworn, because it was his Sabbath. The court, therefore, fined him 10 £; but the defendant, afterwards, waiving the benefit of his testimony, he was discharged from the fine." Stansbury v. Marks, 2 U.S. (2 Dall.) 213 (1793).

Among the cases to reach the Supreme Court of the United States were: Pence v. Langdon, 99 U.S. 578 (1878) (rescission of contract on Sunday); Gibbs & Sterret Mfg. Co. v. Brucker, 111 U.S. 595 (1884) (contract made on Sunday); Bucher v. Cheshire R.R., 125 U.S. 555 (1888) (passenger travelling on Sunday barred from negligence suit against railroad carrier); Ball v. United States, 140 U.S. 118 (1891) (jury verdict on Sunday); Stone v. United States, 167 U.S. 178 (1897) (jury verdict on Sunday). See also Soon Hing v. Crowley, 113 U.S. 703 (1885).

345 64 U.S. (23 How.) 28 (1859).

346 *Id.* at 37.

347 *Id.* at 42. (All italicized in original.)

348 *Id.* at 43.

349 Philadelphia, W. & B. R.R. v. Philadelphia, & Havre de Grace Steam Towboat Co., 64 U.S. (23 How.) 209 (1860).

350 *Id.* at 218.

351 *Id.* at 219.

352 163 U.S. 299 (1896).

353 *Id.* at 304.

354 Church of the Holy Trinity v. United States, 143 U.S. 457, 471 (1892).

355 177 U.S. 164 (1900).

356 *Id.* at 165.

357 *Ibid.*

358 113 U.S. 703 (1885).

359 *Id.* at 710.

360 366 U.S. 420 (1961).

361 *Id.* at 422.

362 *Ibid.*

363 See, *e.g.*, Katz, *Freedom of Religion and State Neutrality*, 20 U. CHI. L. REV. 426 (1953).

364 366 U.S. at 430.

365 *Ibid.*

366 *Id.* at 431.

367 *Id.* at 433–34.

368 *Id.* at 435.

369 *Id.* at 442.

370 *Id.* at 444–45.

371 *Id.* at 448.

372 In distinguishing the *McCollum* case at this point, the Court raised real doubts about the vitality of *Zorach v. Clauson.* See pp. 86-90 *supra.* "In *McCollum*, state action permitted religious instruction in public school buildings during school hours and required students not attending the religious instruction to remain in their classrooms during that time. The Court found that this system had the effect of coercing the children to attend religious classes; no such coercion to attend church services is present in the situation at bar. In *McCollum*, the only alternative available to the nonattending students was to remain in their classrooms; the alternatives open to nonlaboring persons in the instant case are far more diverse. In *McCollum*, there was direct cooperation between state officials and religious ministers; no such direct participation exists under the Maryland laws. In *McCollum*, tax supported buildings were used to aid religion; in the instant case, no tax monies are being used in aid of religion." *Id.* at 452–53.

373 *Id.* at 453.

374 366 U.S. 617 (1961).

375 *Id.* at 627.

376 *Id.* at 630.

377 366 U.S. 599 (1961).

378 Gallagher v. Crown Kosher Super Market, 366 U.S. 617, 631 (1961).

379 366 U.S. 582 (1961). This case was disposed of in an opinion for the Court by Mr. Chief Justice Warren essentially on the same basis as the *McGowan* case. It need not, therefore, be considered any further here.

380 See pp. 21-22 *supra.*

381 See pp. 65-66 *supra.*

382 366 U.S. at 605.

383 *Ibid.*

384 *Id.* at 606.

385 *Id.* at 607.

386 *Id.* at 608.

387 *Id.* at 608–09.

388 Shreveport v. Levy, 26 La. Ann. 671, 672 (1874). See also State v. Haining, 131 Kan. 853, 293 Pac. 762 (1930); Commonwealth v. Has, 122 Mass. 40 (1877); State v. Weiss, 97

Minn. 125, 105 N.W. 1127 (1906); People v. Rudnick, 259 App. Div. 922, 22 N.Y.S.2d 996 (1940); People v. Adler, 174 App. Div. 301, 160 N.Y. Supp. 539 (1916).

389 McGowan v. Maryland, 366 U.S. 420, 459 (1961) (separate opinion).

390 The only opinion of importance omitted from consideration would seem to be that of the English Court of Criminal Appeal in *Rex v. Garvin.* See HERBERT, THE UNCOMMON LAW 13 (6th ed. 1948).

391 See Comment, *Supreme Court No-Clear-Majority Decisions: A Study in Stare Decisis,* 24 U. CHI. L. REV. 99 (1956).

392 366 U.S. at 462.

393 *Id.* at 463.

394 *Id.* at 464.

395 *Id.* at 465–67.

396 *Id.* at 467.

397 *Id.* at 543.

398 *Id.* at 561.

399 See pp. 86-90 *supra.*

400 366 U.S. at 562.

401 *Id.* at 565.

402 *Id.* at 571. The observation of the first day of the week does not derive from *Exodus* but is generally associated with the resurrection of Christ. But this, of course, makes no difference to the argument offered by Mr. Justice Douglas.

403 *Id.* at 578.

404 *Id.* at 574.

405 Braunfeld v. Brown, 366 U.S. 599, 614 (1961) (dissenting opinion).

406 See cases cited note 388 *supra.*

407 367 U.S. 488 (1961).

408 "[N]o religious test ought ever to be required as a qualification for any office or profit or trust in this State, other than a declaration of belief in the existence of God . . . ." MD. CONST. art. 37.

409 223 Md. 49, 162 A.2d 438 (1960).

410 367 U.S. at 494–96.

411 See pp. 21-22 *supra.*

412 See note 43 *supra.*

413 WHITE, THE MAKING OF THE PRESIDENT 1960 (1961).

414 Wechsler, *Toward Neutral Principles of Constitutional Law,* 73 HARV. L. REV. 1 (1959).

415 See, *e.g.,* Miller & Howell, *The Myth of Neutrality in Constitutional Adjudication,* 27 U. CHI. L. REV. 661 (1960).